THE GIFTS UNWRAPPED

How to Know, Identify, And
Operate in the Gifts of the Holy Spirit

Evans Pierre

WESTBOW
PRESS®
A DIVISION OF THOMAS NELSON
& ZONDERVAN

WestBow Press books may be ordered through booksellers or by contacting:

WestBow Press
A Division of Thomas Nelson & Zondervan
1663 Liberty Drive
Bloomington, IN 47403
www.westbowpress.com
1 (866) 928-1240

ISBN: 978-1-5127-2851-4 (sc)
ISBN: 978-1-5127-2852-1 (hc)
ISBN: 978-1-5127-2850-7 (e)

Library of Congress Control Number: 2016901354

Print information available on the last page.

WestBow Press rev. date: 3/30/2016

Contents

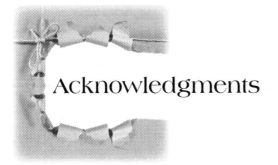

Acknowledgments

I want to first acknowledge and thank the Lord for saving me, and calling me to such a work of glorifying Him and edifying His body. I also want to thank Him for the writing of this book. Without Him, this book would not have been written.

I also want to thank my wife for her encouragement in writing this book. Honey, there are many things I could say, but it will suffice to say here that you are absolutely a blessing. Thanks for the push!

Pastor Powell, by your encouragement through many sermons and your example, this book has come forth. Thank you for your unwavering ministry of encouragement and apostolic covering.

I want to also thank my biological parents, Joseph and Anata Pierre. Because of your lives, I have come to know Christ, and become a servant of His.

To my spiritual parents, Derek and Sheila Davis. You two are amazing. The laughs and straight talks have been a needed blessing. Thank you immensely for your prayers and support.

To my mentees, you all are awesome. You've played a powerful role as to how this book has come to be.

To my Agape Family, what a wonderful assembly! Thank you for the years of service. It has been a blessing, and continues to be as I mature in Christ by serving you all. This book comes as a result of the countless encounters with God as we worship and serve Him together.

Scripture Reference

1 Corinthians 12:7-11

But the manifestation of the Spirit is given to each one for the profit of all: for to one is given the word of wisdom through the Spirit, to another the word of knowledge through the same Spirit, to another faith by the same Spirit, to another gifts of healings by the same Spirit, to another the working of miracles, to another prophecy, to another discerning of spirits, to another different kinds of tongues, to another the interpretation of tongues. But one and the same Spirit works all these things, distributing to each one individually as He wills. (NKJV)

Foreword

I am delighted to commend Evans Pierre to you as a capable minister of the New Testament, a covenant not of written laws but one of the Spirit (2 Corinthians 3:6). Evans loves the Lord Jesus, His Kingdom and the Church of God. Likewise, he enjoys teaching the Word and encouraging others in pursuit of their heavenly assignment. Evans' book, *The Gifts Unwrapped* is congruent with the same.

The gifts of the Holy Spirit have always been a fascinating topic of interest for me. It is truly amazing that God gracefully partners with His beloved children to minister supernaturally with Him. Moreover, beyond study to participating with the Lord to bless others has been personally and deeply fulfilling.

Regretfully, the state of affairs for many regarding spiritual gifts in the Church today is "all hype and no substance." For these individuals, talk is plentiful but results are few. Scripture contends, a person who boasts about a gift that does not exist is like clouds and wind without rain (Proverbs 25:14). In other words, to brag of what one does not have is highly disappointing in that such boasting can never deliver on a promise.

Notwithstanding, for those clearly gifted but ill-informed and inexperienced, today is a day of reckoning. Will you embrace the truth and practice of being "Spirit filled" and "Spirit led" to really living it or choose instead to be indifferent and inactive? I anticipate the former and that reading The Gifts Unwrapped will inspire, challenge and transform the way you think and minister the abilities God has placed within you.

Read the contents of this book prayerfully and expectantly. Prepare to be instructed and so moved to "stir up the gift that is in you" recalling God has not given you "a spirit of fear, but of power and of love and of a sound mind" (1 Timothy 2:6-7).

Furthermore, be sure to do all things in such a way that Jesus Christ's presence may be evident at all times. Do everything to the glory of God rather than for fleshly, selfish reasons. Remember, the wisdom of the old adage, "God may be give you the cash but always give Him the credit." Finally, your faith and obedience will reveal God's manifold grace to a world that so desperately needs to see His glory today. In this the Lord will be pleased.

Grace and Peace,

Lawrence Powell
Agape Family Worship Center | www.agapecenter.org
Rahway, New Jersey

Endorsements

This humble servant of Christ operates in the gifts of the Spirit with precision and accuracy. Elder Pierre is not writing from theory, but from experience. Enjoy this powerful book as he shares insights on the gifts of the Spirit.

- Pastor Dwayne Wright
  Kingdom Living Ministries
  Piscataway, NJ

It is one thing to know and identify the gifts of the Spirit, but it is truly a work of the Holy Spirit to learn and know how to operate in the gifts. In this timeless, comprehensive study, Elder Pierre not only equips the body of Christ with a deeper understanding of the gifts, but he goes a step further and teaches how to operate in the gifts. Elder Pierre unwraps the gifts with biblical truth, wisdom, skill, revelation, and personal experience. *The Gifts Unwrapped* is a must have for those who truly desire to experience the full blessing of knowing, identifying, and operating in the gifts of the Holy Spirit.

- Prophetess Carla R. Palin

Tools are an intricate part of any process. This book consists of vital tools (knowledge) designed to equip the Body of Christ in adequately discerning one's gifting.

- Pastor Marchelle McLeod
  Prophetic Vision Deliverance Ministry Intl.
  Newark, NJ

Elder Evans' book *The Gifts Unwrapped* is a text book. His transparent approach to sharing his own journey of learning to use the gifts of God given to him is refreshing and useful; however, more impressive is the supreme job of teaching and explaining the depth of the gifts of the Holy Spirit that Elder Evans does in this book. The book is systematically structured for learning, honestly written for encouragement, and creatively written for enjoyment. Since every believer is given spiritual gifts, I recommend this book for every believer. *The Gifts Unwrapped* will undoubtedly serve as a launching pad of faith for believers to operate in their God given gifts for the glory of God and the edification of the Church. I am grateful to Elder Evans for allowing God to use him to help the Church demonstrate the power of the Gospel.

- Pastor Donna Mosley
  Balm Church
  Bethlehem, PA

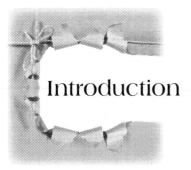

Introduction

Over the years, I have been privileged to serve God's people through the gifts of the Spirit. It is living life on the edge. I have witnessed God do incredible things as He would have me minister to His people. It truly has been thrilling, but my testimony did not start off that way. Thus, the writing of this book.

My Christian experience begins with me growing up in a traditional Baptist congregation, which did not believe in the gifts of the Spirit. My knowledge of these things through my denomination were that God ceased to work in this manner. The time or era for those things had come to an end by the death of the apostles in the first century. Furthermore, there was no need for them, because the Bible is perfect through the canonization of Scripture. Thus, the gifts of the Spirit were simply to get the Church started and moving towards the fulfillment of getting the Gospel to the nations, which is actually the doctrine of many cessationists. Cessationists believe three main points regarding the gifts:

1. The gifts provided supernatural confirmation of the apostolic authority of the early church.
2. They helped lay the foundation for the Church.

3. They gave assistance to the first century saints regarding the work of world evangelism.

This was my foundation, and God used my Baptist denomination to plant a love for the Scriptures. He also placed a wonderful spiritual father to help me during that time in leading me into the reality of the baptism with the Holy Spirit. This started me on my journey of realizing there was so much more that my Baptist denomination did not teach due to their lack of knowledge and erroneous teachings rooted in tradition. Not all was bad, but much was lacking regarding a proper knowledge of the Holy Spirit and His ministry.

I began to study Scripture regarding the teaching after a few weeks. I also attended Bible Study, where we were taught about the baptism with the Holy Spirit. It was illuminating and refreshing. Not too long after that, I received the baptism with the Holy Spirit in my bedroom, but wasn't sure that was the experience. So, I went to my spiritual father at the time, and he prayed over me with the laying on of hands. It was a wonderful moment in my life as we both prayed in the Spirit.

Interestingly enough, things began to happen after receiving the baptism with the Spirit. My spiritual life went up a notch. I was a young preacher, and I immediately recognized a significant change occurred after receiving the baptism. My preaching was more fiery and powerful. My mind was sharper in regards to preaching and teaching the Word. Furthermore, I started to experience a phenomenon where I would lay hands upon individuals and they would "fall". I could not understand it back then, but I do now! It was the anointing of the Spirit and the glory of God.

Other things began to happen that were very exciting, but I was unsure or uncertain regarding them. I would pray for people, and then find myself giving words (i.e., words of prophecy). People would then ask me afterwards, "How did you know those things?" Then, I started to hear a voice. Later on I discovered it was the voice of God. I have come to know His voice intimately. It is a treasured thing for me personally. There's nothing like when you know you've heard Him, and see the reality of what He said come to pass. It's simply amazing! I began to know that God was experientially real! Not only is He a transcendent being, but one who is truly near.

I then started to experience other realities – the gifts of the Spirit. Some manifested in my life more than others. Later on I would come to understand why – my calling. Your calling bears various gifts for the necessity of fulfilling it. Prophet Dennis Cramer states, "Supernatural gifts point to your supernatural calling. Discover your current arsenal, your present inventory of spiritual gifts, and you will often discover your greater calling." (*The Master's Call*, p. 95)

Now I must say that through the process of experiencing all these graces of God, I made many mistakes. I fell down a lot, but I would get back up (Proverbs 24:16). There were times I wanted to give up on my calling and gifts, but someone in me would not let me – the Holy Spirit (1 John 4:4, Romans 11:29).

Over the years I have matured in my character and gifting, and I am ever grateful for the journey. Because of having gone through all I have and due to the particular call of God upon my life, which is to equip and edify believers for effective ministry, I have taken the liberty of writing this book to do just that in relation to the gifts.

I have been privileged to minister through preaching and holding training sessions for believers over the years, and I have been asked various questions. I thought that this would help many to understand what the gifts are in nature, how to identify them when they manifest, and how to operate in them towards effectiveness in producing the desired results as shown in Scripture.

My prayer is that God will help you the reader to gain insight and a greater appreciation of what Christ has made available to us through His substitutionary work at the cross, through the agency of His Spirit in accomplishing the fulfillment of the Great Commission, and by reason of your calling. I further pray that this book will not merely grant you the reader insight, but inspire you to move out into operating in the gifts of the Spirit. May the Lord richly bless you as you read!

Chapter 1

Hebrews 2:4

At the same time, God also testified by signs and wonders, various miracles, and distributions of gifts from the Holy Spirit according to His will. (HCSB)

As we approach this study upon the gifts of the Holy Spirit, I first want to address the nature of the gifts. When one looks at the nature of the gifts, the question one has to ask is "What are they?" The gifts of the Spirit, in nature, are several things. **The gifts are supernatural, gifts from our Heavenly Father, tools, weapons, treasures of heaven, and a witness of our Lord.** Let us take a look at each one of them.

Supernatural in Nature

The gifts of the Holy Spirit by nature are not natural, but supernatural. What I mean here is that these gifts are not things that one can acquire by natural means over a durable length of time. One cannot go to seminary or Bible school to acquire their presence in one's life. The gifts are given by a supernatural Being, and He is the

Holy Spirit. As the Holy Spirit is a supernatural being, so are the gifts supernatural.

Being supernatural, the gifts are not limited in their expression in the earth. In the word supernatural, you find "super-", and it means "to be above or beyond". Therefore, the gifts are above or beyond the natural realm of existence. They supersede the limitations of this world. They are not governed by the dictates of the limitations of this present age, for they are from an age that is to come (Hebrews 6:4-5). They are bound by laws beyond the laws of this plain of existence, and they reflect the nature of a Supreme Being – God. Therefore, the gifts are a sign, which point to the Holy Spirit. The gifts reveal that the Holy Spirit is God.

Gifts

The gifts of the Holy Spirit are just that – gifts. When one receives a gift, it is given based upon the goodness or kindness of the giver. The gifts are given to us by a supernatural God based upon His supreme goodness towards us. The gifts are not given based upon the merit of the receiver. If it was based upon the receiver, then many believers would be found to be exempt from receiving the gifts of the Holy Spirit. However, this is the glory of the Lord in relation to the gifts. We are recipients of His gifts by virtue of the righteousness of Christ. Because of the intermediary ministry of Jesus at the cross, we have been made righteous. All the sins we ever committed have been erased as if we had never committed them before.

When God looks at us, He sees righteousness. More than that, we are the very righteousness of God in the earth. How is that even possible? Where did this righteousness come from? Again, it came from Christ Himself. As Christ bore our sin, He gave us His righteousness to bear. Therefore, the gifts of the Spirit come by way of righteousness – the righteousness of Christ.

Tools

The gifts of the Spirit are tools for the edifying or building up of the Body of Christ. Paul writes to the Corinthian assembly stating we (i.e., the Universal Church) are the temple of the Holy Spirit (1 Corinthians 3:16). Therefore, as Spirit-filled believers use the gifts, or give expression to the work and ministry of the Holy Spirit by the gifts, they bring about the furtherance of the construction of the temple of God. However, a tool within the hand of a novice is a dangerous thing. Paul, in Romans 10:2, states, **"I can testify about them that they have zeal for God, but not according to knowledge."** (HCSB) So, we need instruction to better understand the gifts. This is one of the major reasons for this book – to help believers gain knowledge and understanding regarding the gifts of the Holy Spirit.

Weapons

Paul states in 2 Corinthians 10:3-5 that we have been given weapons of mass destruction. The gifts of the Spirit are part of this arsenal of weaponry. The purpose of these weapons are for the tearing down of demonic strongholds. As the gifts are in operation, demonic strongholds are demolished, and spiritual captives are set free. We need to understand that the gifts are powerful. When we move in alignment to that understanding, we will see the might of God and His kingdom show forth in brilliance against the kingdom of darkness. The gifts are needed and are an asset in spiritual warfare.

Treasures of Heaven

The gifts of the Holy Spirit are treasures of Heaven. I gained this insight from Genesis twenty four where Eliezer was sent of Abraham to seek a bride for Isaac. This Old Testament account is full of insightful teaching regarding the ministry of the Godhead (God the Father, God the Son, and God the Holy Spirit), and the present interrelationship of Christ and His Bride (i.e., the Church). To truly see what I am going to share here regarding the gifts, I must give some typological references of the individuals within the account. Abraham is a type of God the Father, Isaac is a type of God the Son, Eliezer is a type of God the Holy Spirit, and Rebekah is a type of the Church.

With this understanding, let us look at verses forty five to sixty, for they help us to understand how the gifts are treasures. Eliezer is sitting by the well praying, and here comes Rebekah in answer to his prayers. Eliezer perceives that Rebekah is the bride whom God has chosen to be wife for his master Isaac, and then after he worships, he does something profound. In verse fifty three, Eliezer places jewelry of silver and gold, and various precious things upon her. He did this to identify her now as the chosen bride of the promised son.

As we have established the types, we can see that when we receive the Holy Spirit, He brings with Himself treasures and precious things. The gifts of the Spirit are part of those treasures from on high, which the Holy Spirit puts upon our spirit to identify us as Christ's Bride, but also to set us apart as servants that will supernaturally serve the purposes of the kingdom of God as the Bride of Christ (Genesis 2:20). The gifts of the Holy Spirit are emanations of the glory of God, so that the nations may see God's goodness toward humanity

(Ezekiel 16:14). Therefore, we ought to proudly wear the gifts, so that all men may see and hear of God's goodness through Jesus Christ by the powerful presence of the Holy Spirit.

A Witness of the Lord

The final thing regarding the nature of the gifts is that they are a testimony of the present ministry of Christ. He is presently alive in the heavenly tabernacle of God. The author of Hebrews helps us to understand that Jesus is our High Priest (Hebrews 3:1, 4:14, 6:20). In the Old Testament, the high priest was required to wear bells at the hem of the priestly ephod (Exodus 28:31-33). The purpose of the bells were to make a sound to be heard from within the Sanctuary as an indication to those outside he was still alive. If the bells were not heard, then it meant that the priest had died, and God had not honored his ministry nor received his sacrifice.

Our High Priest has gone beyond the veil of the natural cosmos to appear on our behalf, so as to sprinkle His blood upon the altar of God. How do we know God the Father has honored the ministry and accepted the sacrifice of Jesus? Luke writes in Acts 2:2 saying, **"Suddenly, there was a sound from heaven"**. (NLT) The descent of the Spirit at Pentecost is the evidential proof that Christ's ministry was honored, His sacrifice was accepted, and the result being the forgiveness of our sins. Therefore, when the gifts of the Spirit are in operation, they testify to the validity of Christ's present resurrected state, and His power still operative in the earth by the Person of the Holy Spirit.

We have just briefly looked at what the gifts of the Spirit are, and to reiterate, they are supernatural in nature, gifts, tools, weapons, treasures of heaven, and a witness of our Lord's substitutionary ministry at the cross and present priestly ministry in heaven. We now see that the gifts are important realities in the Church, and assets that we must not despise.

In the next chapter, I will deal with Cessationism, and then move to address an aspect the apostle Paul presents regarding the gifts of the Spirit – manifestation. Then, I will progress in the following chapters to give the groupings of the gifts for ease of understanding, and then define and describe each gift. Throughout the book, I will endeavor to give my own personal testimony in relation to the gifts of the Spirit, and share testimonials of people who have been impacted by the ministry of the Holy Spirit.

Chapter 2

An Active Presence

But the manifestation of the Spirit is given to each one for the profit of all... (1 Corinthians 12:7, NKJV)

In 1 Corinthians, we find that Paul has been addressing various issues within the Corinthian assemblies. As an apostle, he is seeking to establish order within the Church in Corinth (1 Corinthians 14:33). He has addressed matters of schism, immorality, and now in chapter twelve he is addressing the matter that involves the gifts of the Spirit. He is bringing correction and establishing order in relation to them, so that there is no demonic activity under the guise of Christian spirituality.

Before we deal with the listing of the gifts, I want to address here their relevance. Why is this study relevant? To cessationists, this portion of Scripture is merely historical in nature, and has no continuous present experiential reality to the 21st century Church. The reason being is due to their understanding of the gifts. Cessationists believe these gifts have ceased with the passing away of the 1st century apostles and saints. Their proof text is 1 Corinthians 13:8-10.

1 Corinthians 13:8-10

> **Love never fails [never fades out or becomes obsolete or comes to an end]. As for prophecy (the gift of interpreting the divine will and purpose), it will be fulfilled and pass away; as for tongues, they will be destroyed and cease; as for knowledge, it will pass away [it will lose its value and be superseded by truth]. For our knowledge is fragmentary (incomplete and imperfect), and our prophecy (our teaching) is fragmentary (incomplete and imperfect). But when the complete and perfect (total) comes, the incomplete and imperfect will vanish away (become antiquated, void, and superseded).** (AMP)

However, this text does not prove the doctrine of cessation in the true sense of the text here. Let us look at what this text really means. The key to understanding the text is found in the word "perfect". What is Paul referring to when he uses the term?

Cessationists believe that the "perfect" here points to the canonized Bible. Their reasoning is since the Bible has been canonized, spiritual knowledge is perfect. There is no more need for prophecy, tongues, and the other gifts listed in first Corinthians twelve. They look at prophecy as likened to the prophetic writings (i.e., the prophetic books, such as Isaiah, Jeremiah, Ezekiel, and the Minor Prophets), which became Scripture. What they do not realize is there were prophecies that were recorded not for the purpose of doctrine, but for the present effective ministry of the Church.

Acts 11:27-30

> **In those days some prophets came down from Jerusalem to Antioch. Then one of them, named Agabus, stood up**

and predicted by the Spirit that there would be a severe famine throughout the Roman world. This took place during the time of Claudius. So each of the disciples, according to his ability, determined to send relief to the brothers who lived in Judea. They did this, sending it to the elders by means of Barnabas and Saul. (HCSB)

Some prophecies were given during the days of the early Church, but were not recorded.

Acts 15:30-32

So when they were sent away, they went down to Antioch; and having gathered the congregation together, they delivered the letter. When they had read it, they rejoiced because of its encouragement. Judas and Silas, also being prophets themselves, encouraged and strengthened the brethren with a lengthy [prophetic] message. (NASB)

Prophecy was not only intended for ministerial purposes, but for the edification, exhortation, and comfort of the believers as the apostle Paul notes in 1 Corinthians 12:3.

Let us now look at what the word "perfect" meant here in this passage of 1 Corinthians 13. The Greek word for perfect here is teleios (Strong's Concordance #5046), and when looking at the references that show the use of telos or teleios, all are related to the return of Christ and the end times (1 Corinthians 1:8, 15:24, James 5:7-8, Revelation 20:4, 5, 7, 21:6, 22:13). "Perfect" relates to a set time, unknown to the Church, yet known by God alone. This "perfect" time is the return of the Lord Jesus Christ! Prophecy, tongues, and all the others gifts of the Spirit will **cease** when the Lord returns. Why? Paul helps us by explaining why in the following Scripture.

1 Corinthians 13:11-12

> **When I was a child, I used to speak like a child, think like a child, reason like a child; when I became a man, I did away with childish things. For now we see in a mirror dimly, but then face to face; now I know in part, but then I will know fully just as I also have been fully known.** (NASB)

We need the gifts in this present time, but when Christ ushers us into the age that is to come, there will be no need for the gifts. We will be with Him, and know Him as we are known. Therefore, the gifts are needed today as they were centuries before, and they are still to be in operation in our present modern day context.

Another portion of Scripture that helps us to understand this as well is this next portion of Scripture.

1 Corinthians 1:4-8

> **I thank my God always about you, in respect of the grace of God given to you in Christ Jesus; that in everything ye have been enriched in him, in all word of doctrine, and all knowledge, (according as the testimony of the Christ has been confirmed in you,) so that ye come short in no [spiritual] gift, awaiting the revelation of our Lord Jesus Christ; who shall also confirm you to the end, unimpeachable in the day of our Lord Jesus Christ.** (DBY)

Did you see it?

"Ye come short in no [spiritual] gift, awaiting the revelation of our Lord Jesus Christ."

Powerful declaration! The gifts are not to fall short or suffer want in any part of their expression and operation, but to increase as we wait for the return of the Lord Jesus Christ. There is cessation, but not as the Cessationists believe as noted in chapter one. There will be a continuation **until** the return of the Lord.

In *2000 Years of Charismatic Christianity* by Eddie L Hyatt, the author helps us to see that the gifts of the Spirit truly continued beyond the first apostles of the church, and carried throughout the centuries. The words of the apostle rings true!

We need to address one other aspect in regards to the gifts as they are today in comparison to the first century saints. Are the gifts in the manner whereby prophecy is on the same level as Scripture, such as the Old Testament prophets? Absolutely not! Furthermore, to use as an example, are apostles of today on the same level as the apostles of the 1st century who walked with our Lord? Of course not! The apostles of the first century were afforded a privilege that the apostles of our present day are not:

1. They saw the Lord Jesus in bodily form.
2. They received direct instruction from the Lord.
3. They received the Spirit directly from Him.
4. They saw Him personally/bodily work miracles.
5. Some of them wrote authoritative documents (i.e., epistles) which became canonized Scripture (2 Peter 3:16).

However, there is a connectivity that modern day apostles have with the original first century apostles. The modern day apostles are called into their office by the Holy Spirit as seen in the following example.

Acts 13:1–3

> **Now in the church at Antioch there were prophets and teachers: Barnabas, Simeon called Niger, Lucius of Cyrene, Manaen (who had been brought up with Herod the tetrarch) and Saul. While they were worshiping the Lord and fasting, the Holy Spirit said, "Set apart for me Barnabas and Saul for the work to which I have called them." So after they had fasted and prayed, they placed their hands on them and sent them off.** (NIV)

And there is more...

1. They have the same Holy Spirit who worked in the 1st century apostles. (Acts 9:17)
2. Their authoritative office is still to be a present reality. (Acts 1:20b, Act 13:2)
3. They retain the very same anointing. (2 Corinthians 1:21)
4. They are still called to plant churches. (1 Corinthians 3:6a)
5. They are called to have oversight over those churches as loving fathers over their children to train and develop in love. (1 Corinthians 4:15)
6. They carry revelation. (2 Corinthians 12:1)
7. They have a burden for the Church and the churches they plant. (Romans 1:9-12, 2 Corinthians 11:28)
8. They have a distinct ability to preach/teach the word of God. (Acts 5:42)
9. They have a sphere of influence. (i.e., a network of churches, ministries, etc.)
10. They have an arsenal of miraculous gifts: gift of faith, gift of healings, working of miracles.

11. They have a grace to endure hardships. (2 Corinthians 11:22-27, 12:12)

12. They are a sort of compass for the Church. (2 Corinthians 10:3-8, Ephesians 4:11-13)

13. They bring fresh air or insight from heaven. (1 Corinthians 14:26)

14. They are trailblazers – always seeking to chart new courses for the Church. (Acts 16:6-10)

Let us now look at 1 Corinthians 12:7, which is a transitional point in the letter where the apostle begins to list the gifts of the Spirit. In listing the gifts, he uses an interesting word or term to relate to the gifts – manifestation.

The term "manifestation", in verse seven, is the Greek word phanerōsis (Strong's Concordance #5321). It simply means "to make something

> **When the gifts are in operation, you are witnessing the manifestation of God in the earth.**

clearly seen and known". Whenever the gifts are in operation, the Spirit is making Himself clearly seen and known. When there is an authentic working of the Spirit in relation to the gifts, there is no mistake, you have just witnessed a manifestation of God in the earth!

Let us look at the next thing here in regards to the gifts, and that is the gifts are given. This is a powerful statement, and one that needs to be explained.

First, the gifts are according to grace. Grace defined means "unmerited favor". Grace is the loving kindness shown by a good and merciful God through Christ Jesus in which could not otherwise be received by any human action in relation to a merit system. If the gifts are in operation in you, it is not due to your own merit or goodness, but the goodness and mercy of God towards you because of the merit of Christ. Hence, the gifts are called "grace gifts".

Also, these grace gifts operate on the same basis as to when you were saved – grace through faith (Romans 10:17, 12:3, Ephesians 2:8). Grace came by way of the portal of faith. The gifts operate through the same portal. One major reason many within the body of Christ are not experiencing the gifts is due to a misunderstanding of faith and a works related mindset. Those who are operating in the gifts are those who have learned to approach them as children, and they are maturing in that spiritual mindset and experiencing greater measure of the gifts of the Spirit. We will look at this a little more later on in the book.

Another thing to note, the Holy Spirit uses those who are available. Regardless of what is going on, or who may be present, available believers say, "Use me Lord! Send me Lord! I'll go, say, and do whatever it is You will." If that is your posture, get ready, for you're going to experience the gifts in your life.

As mentioned previously, these gifts are given. They are given not on the grounds of works or merit, but on the grounds of grace through faith. Any Spirit-filled believer can operate in the gifts, but this word captures a greater meaning. There are those who are given gifts as a permanent reality to operate within their Christian life and service (Acts 21:9). It is likened to a deposit made by the Spirit in regards to your calling and function within the Church.

Romans 11:29

God's gracious gifts and calling are irrevocable. (HCSB)

Furthermore, each Spirit-filled believer has received at least one spiritual gift (Acts 21:9). Yet, you can have more than one gift, and that is determined by the Spirit as noted in verse 1 Corinthians 12:11, **"But one and the same Spirit is active in all these, distributing to each person as He wills."** (HCSB) Others who do have multiple gifts many a times are those within the five-fold ministry gifts (ascension gifts – Ephesians 4:8, 11). As an example, a prophet has the gifts of prophecy, word of knowledge, word of wisdom, and discerning of spirits. These are primary, and are considered the prophetic gifts.

The question that is often asked, "How does one know which gift one has?" Whenever something is deposited, there is evidence. There is a record or receipt made for a deposit. Therefore, there is evidential proof by virtue of a track record in your life. You know what gift you have by virtue of its **repetitive use**, and its **Biblical goal** being met. If there is no repetitive use, then one must question if he or she has been given a specific gift on a permanent basis in relation to one's calling.

This brings me to the final point of this verse – the Biblical goal is "the profit of all". The goal that God endeavors upon in the use of the gifts is "profit".

Jeremiah 23:32

> **Behold, I am against them that prophesy false dreams, sayeth the LORD, and do tell them, and cause my people to err by their lies, and by their lightness; yet I sent them not, nor commanded them: therefore they shall not profit this people at all, sayeth the LORD.** (KJV).

When you define the word profit, you get that the word means to advance, to have an advantage, to benefit, and to progress. When the gifts are used, they cause the person on the receiving end to receive something that enables them to move beyond where they are to a more advantageous state, condition, place, and/or point. It further means to rise above obstacles, and to produce effective outcomes. Whenever the gifts manifest, the Holy Spirit is granting the recipient favor. That person is experiencing the kindness of the Father towards them, which translates into them being enabled to profit.

Luke 11:11-13

> **What father among you, if his son asks for a loaf of bread, will give him a stone; or if he asks for a fish, will instead of a fish give him a serpent? Or if he asks for an egg, will give him a scorpion? If you then, evil as you are, know how to give good gifts [gifts that are to their advantage] to your children, how much more will your heavenly Father give the Holy Spirit to those who ask and continue to ask Him!** (AMP)

The gifts bring about an edge to the person ministering, and the recipient of the supernatural or gifted ministry. This is why Satan fights so hard against the gifts. It is an advantage over him and his kingdom. We must, as Paul states, **"Desire the gifts − eagerly pursue and seek to acquire [this] love [make it your aim, your great quest]; and earnestly desire and cultivate the spiritual endowments (gifts), especially that you may prophesy (interpret the divine will and purpose in inspired preaching and teaching)."** (1 Corinthians 14:1, AMP)

The gifts are part of the Church's arsenal and weaponry against the kingdom of darkness (2 Corinthians 10:3-5). They are spiritual, and they are powerful. The gifts are profitable to the Church, but destructive to the kingdom of Satan. Let's not give into false beliefs that teach and seek to persuade us to give up on the gifts. We will hold fast to the writings of the apostle Paul in the following verse.

1 Thessalonians 5:19–20

> **Do not quench (suppress or subdue) the [Holy] Spirit; do not spurn the gifts and utterances of the prophets [do not depreciate prophetic revelations nor despise inspired instruction or exhortation or warning].** (AMP)

Now, in chapters 3–11, I will begin to outline the gifts, their groupings, define them, and give descriptions for them. For where there are examples for the gifts, I will endeavor to give an Old Testament and New Testament biblical reference. As mentioned previously, I will also attempt to give personal testimony from my experience with the gifts over the years, and share testimonials from others who have received ministry from me by the Holy Spirit. Chapters 12–14 will cover the final part of this book, which is on how to operate in the gifts of the Spirit.

Chapter 3

The Word of Wisdom

For to one is given the word of wisdom through the Spirit...
(I Corinthians 12:8, NKJV)

In this chapter, I want to first list the gifts in their groupings.

There are nine gifts, and they can be grouped into three groups for simplicity:

1.   The **revelation** gifts – they **reveal** something
2.   The **power** gifts – they **do** something
3.   The **vocal** gifts – they **say** something

Let's also list the gifts in their groupings:

1.   The **revelation** gifts:

    a.   Word of wisdom

    b.   Word of knowledge

    c.   Discerning of spirits

2. The **power** gifts

    a.   Gift of faith

    b.   Gifts of healings

    c.   Working of miracles

3. The **vocal** gifts

    a.   Gift of prophecy

    b.   Gift of different kinds of tongues

    c.   Gift of interpretation of tongues

Each of these gifts are supernatural in nature, and they do something that profits (i.e., benefits, helps, assists, gives an advantage, an edge) believers, and at times, even sinners towards a relationship with God. Of course, after any of these gifts, a verbal presentation of the Gospel should follow. You will see this interplay of proclamation and demonstration throughout the Gospels and in the book of Acts. In regards to evangelism, supernatural demonstration should never stand alone, but be followed by a verbal proclamation to help the nonbeliever receive Christ as their Lord and Savior through repentance and faith (Mark 1:15).

In the first grouping, which is the revelation gifts, the first noted is the word of wisdom. The next is the power gifts, and the first mentioned is the gift of faith. The last grouping is the vocal gifts, and the first mentioned in that grouping is the gift of prophecy. The first of the groups shows the primacy (first in rank) over the other gifts. The word of wisdom is superior in rank to that of the word of knowledge. The same principle goes for the other groups.

We will see how these gifts function synergistically. When they work together, they produce a powerful and marvelous output. Truly the person that receives such ministry will profit.

Now, let's look at the first gift – word of wisdom. Remember, these gifts are supernatural in nature. This gift is not natural or even worldly wisdom (James 3:15). This is not wisdom that is under the sun (Ecclesiastes 2:19), but over and beyond the sun. This is not wisdom that is learned over time. It is not even wisdom that comes through the study of Scripture.

To define this gift, Derek Prince states, the gift "is a tiny portion of God's total wisdom directly and supernaturally imparted by the Holy Spirit." This wisdom is like what Paul describes as a "spirit of wisdom and revelation" (Ephesians 1:17). This is a wisdom that comes by way of revelation. This is wisdom that finds its origin in God, on the spot, given for the right thing, at the right time/moment, and at the right place. It is not learned nor rehearsed, but grasped in a moment by the human spirit through the agency of the Holy Spirit.

Consequently, this wisdom is specific to a person's set of circumstances. It is not vague or general. It is not around the ball park, but it is very much direct, and comes with a sense of great conviction of its certainty. There is a boldness in its delivery.

This wisdom is directional. It gives the person applicable things to do. When this gift is in operation, the person is not in the dark as to what they are to do. They know God has given them specific direction in light of their situation. They have ammunition now to face whatever the challenge is.

The word of wisdom is futuristic or predictive in nature. This gift addresses what will happen in the future, and how one is to conduct themselves in light of that futuristic occurrence. This gift is unlike the next gift we will discuss in the next chapter, which is the word of knowledge.

Now, let us look at some Scriptural references in light of this gift.

Genesis 41:15–39

Due to the length of the reference, please take this moment to read the passage before moving on in the chapter.

In the passage, we see that Pharaoh has a divinely inspired prophetic message in the form of two dreams, but he is unable to discern their meaning. So he seeks all those who were within his court to gain insight of what the troublesome dreams could mean. They were unable to discern their meaning either, because divinely inspired dreams or visions can only be discerned by the assistance of the Spirit of God (1 Corinthians 2:14).

You know the story from the text, Joseph is summoned, and he directly tells Pharaoh that God is the only one who can interpret his dreams. Notice something; the source of interpretation of divinely inspired dreams and visions is God! Let us follow what Pharaoh states as written by the author of Genesis – **"Can we find anyone else like this man so obviously filled with the spirit of God?"** (Genesis 41:38, NLT) The Spirit of God! Joseph said, "God", and pharaoh attributes the manifestation of this gift of wisdom to the "Spirit of God".

Another thing to note is that the word of wisdom is an answer of peace. Whenever the word of wisdom manifests, it answers something that was troubling a person. This answer of peace in the form of this gift was such a help to Pharaoh that he made Joseph second-in-command in Egypt.

Notice how the gift came into manifestation. It came following the interpretation. It was linked to a supernatural gift. Some will say that it was a natural ability of discernment, but it was linked by the supernatural gift. It is not likened to when Moses' father-in-law gave advice, but this was in the same supernatural vein. He gave the meaning, and then followed it up with wisdom, and all by supernatural means.

The result was that the whole nation was spared of a disastrous famine that would have decimated the whole land economically, territorially, and a great number of the populace. There would have been great loss, but this word of wisdom spared them all. The word of wisdom was **specific** (to the situation), **directional** (what Pharaoh needed to do), and **predictive** (dealt with the future).

Let's turn to another example found in the Old Testament. This one is the product of Samuel ministering prophetically to the soon to be chosen king (Saul).

1 Samuel 10:1-9

> **Samuel took the flask of oil, poured it out on Saul's head kissed him, and said, "Hasn't the LORD anointed you ruler over His inheritance? Today when you leave me, you'll find two men at Rachel's Grave at Zelzah in the land of Benjamin. They will say to you, 'The donkeys you went looking for have been found and now your father has stopped being concerned about the donkeys and is worried about you, asking: What should I do about my son?' "You will proceed from there until you come to the oak of Tabor. Three men going up to God at Bethel will meet you there, one bringing three goats, one bringing three loaves**

of bread, and one bringing a skin of wine. They will ask how you are and give you two loaves of bread, which you will accept from them. **The Spirit of the LORD will control you, you will prophesy with them and you will be transformed into a different person. When these signs have happened to you, do whatever your circumstances require because God is with you. Afterward, go ahead of me to Gilgal. I will come to you to offer burnt offerings and to sacrifice fellowship offerings. Wait seven days until I come to you and show you what to do." When Saul turned around to leave Samuel, God changed his heart, and all the signs came about that day.** (HCSB)

Here we find Samuel anointing Saul prophetically as king. He then continues ministering to him prophetically by giving him a word of wisdom, which again is directional, specific, and predictive. I believe that he did this to help establish and build the faith of Saul to know that God had established him as king, and that God would be with him.

John 21:1-7

After this, Jesus revealed Himself again to His disciples by the Sea of Tiberias. He revealed Himself in this way: Simon Peter, Thomas (called "Twin"), Nathanael from Cana of Galilee, Zebedee's sons, and two others of His disciples were together. "I'm going fishing," Simon Peter said to them. "We're coming with you," they told him. They went out and got into the boat, but that night they caught nothing. When

daybreak came, Jesus stood on the shore. However, the disciples did not know it was Jesus. "Men," Jesus called to them, "you don't have any fish, do you?" "No," they answered. "Cast the net on the right side of the boat," He told them, "and you'll find some." So they did, and they were unable to haul it in because of the large number of fish. Therefore the disciple, the one Jesus loved, said to Peter, "It is the Lord!" When Simon Peter heard that it was the Lord, he tied his outer garment around him (for he was stripped) and plunged into the sea. (HCSB)

Here we are seeing the word of wisdom again in the life and ministry of Jesus. The disciples had been out fishing, all night, but caught nothing by the time morning came. Jesus comes along, and by the word of wisdom, tells them what they are to do specifically with a predictive slant, and the result was two-fold: they caught a great load of fish, but most importantly, they recognized the Lord after His resurrection. What was it that caused them to recognize Him? It was in the use of the gift, for Christ did this unto them earlier in His ministry (Luke 5:1-11). It was this gift that drew Peter to leave all and follow Christ. So, He uses the gift to call them back to Himself. Peter, especially, for we see Christ later in the text having a conversation of "Do you love Me?" Jesus was restoring Peter, and the use of the gift was the dramatic start of the process.

SUMMARY

The gift of the word of wisdom is:

1. A supernatural gift.
2. A small portion of God's overall wisdom.
3. Specific to a situation.
4. Directional.
5. Predictive.
6. Not learned over time.
7. Received in a moment.

Chapter 4

The Word of Knowledge

To another the word of knowledge through the same Spirit...
(1 Corinthians 12:8, NKJV)

Last chapter, we looked at the supernatural gift of the word of wisdom. It is a supernatural gift through a Spirit-filled believer relaying a specific, directional, and predictive word. The word of wisdom stems from God who is the All-Wise-God. Since He is the All-Wise-God, He possesses all wisdom. Therefore, the wisdom that is imparted is a portion of the wisdom of God. Furthermore, we saw that this gift is likened to what Paul described in Ephesians 1:18, "a spirit of wisdom and revelation". This gift operates "on the spot". It is not a rehearsed word, nor is it learned over a period of time. This is wisdom that is given at the moment when it is needed.

We turn to the next gift in the grouping of the revelation gifts being "the word of knowledge". Before we begin to define the gift, let us first establish that this gift is supernatural in nature. It is not knowledge that you learn over a period of time. It is knowledge that comes by way of revelation – the Holy Spirit revealing facts.

Different Types of Knowledge

There are different types of knowledge that we must understand, so that we can explain this distinctive gift of the Holy Spirit.

1. Earthly knowledge – the rudimentary principles of this world, such as the things one obtains through secular training through the various grade levels of education.

2. Satanic knowledge, such as the occult writings, which many in Wicca hold to and use to practice their sorcery. This knowledge, one would do well to stay away as far as possible.

3. Biblical knowledge that is learned from the Holy Scriptures.

Let us now begin to define the gift of knowledge.

This gift begins with "a word". We have captured what that means – "a tiny portion". The principle applies here with the gift of the word of knowledge. Let me state it here that God is the All-Knowing-God. He is all-knowing at all times in every place. His knowledge is pervasive and profound. Since that is the case, He is always able to meet **whatever challenge, at whatever time,** and **in whatever place.**

The Omni's of God:

God is Omniscient – All knowing

God is Omnipotent – All powerful

God is Omnipresent – All present or present everywhere (at all times)

Having this understanding, the word of knowledge stems from this reality of the knowledge of God. God grants a Spirit-filled believer a portion of His knowledge from the storehouse of His essence. It is always a brief summation of a past or present fact. Sometimes, the word of knowledge may be a long version of the description of a situation (i.e., the Holy Spirit gives a bit more detail regarding the facts), but the intent is to give as much information or insight regarding facts to effectively minister to a person.

This gift helps people come to the awareness of the existence of God: "If God exists, surely He is knowledgeable of my circumstance." The gift imparts faith to the hearer, but it also helps along the faith of the minister while ministering to the hearer. Faith is critical in this whole process of operating in the supernatural. Why? Because, the minister and the hearer begins to connect with the truth that "If God is this knowledgeable of such personal information (omniscient), surely then He has the ability to do whatever it is that is required (omnipotent)."

When this gift is in operation, it always signals another gift will come into play to assist. While the word of wisdom can stand upon its own, the word of knowledge usually cannot. This gift is always assisted by another gift, because this gift simply informs the hearer that God is aware of the facts. That's it! Knowledge is information, and knowledge is a key! Thus, just as a key unlocks doors of opportunity, so does this gift. It unlocks other gifts that give way to the opportunity for God to do something.

So, at times what you'll notice following this gift is the word of wisdom. The word of knowledge is informational in nature while the word of wisdom is directional in nature. The one informs while the other directs. At other times, the word of knowledge will be accompanied by the gifts of healings. The word of knowledge reveals a medical condition, and then the gifts of healings comes into play to bring the healing needful to rectify what has been revealed.

The word of knowledge is a powerful gift, but it is a limited gift, which requires assistance in order for it to be of any use. It is a gift that leads out the other gift(s) needful to produce the change to a person's circumstance. It is a fountainhead gift. It is the tip of an arrow type gift. It starts off, but the other gifts finish the job.

Now, let us look at some references of this gift in operation.

1 Samuel 9:18-20

> **Then Saul approached Samuel in the gate and said, "Please tell me where the seer's house is." Samuel answered Saul and said, "I am the seer. Go up before me to the high place, for you shall eat with me today; and in the morning I will let you go, and will tell you all that is on your mind. "As for your donkeys which were lost three days ago, do not set your mind on them, for they have been found. And for whom is all that is desirable in Israel? Is it not for you and for all your father's household?" (NASB)**

In this example, we find the prophet Samuel ministering prophetically to the soon to be anointed King Saul. Saul is seeking

> The gifts of the Spirit will operate in ways that you will not expect. Always be open and available to the Holy Spirit.

Samuel to receive prophetic assistance in finding his father's donkeys. Saul asks Samuel if he is the seer, and Samuel responds that he is. Before Saul can ask Samuel regarding his father's donkeys, Samuel directs him to go to the high place for a special meal. He tells him that he will tell him all the desires of his heart. It seems that there were things that God had been laying on Saul's heart, but he was uncertain of their authenticity. Prophetic ministry is such a powerful thing, because it helps bring clarity to the will of God for a life. In the midst of this comes the word of knowledge. Saul never got a chance to share regarding the donkeys, but the word of knowledge comes forth in the midst of the prophetic discourse. That is the nature of this gift. It just seems to pop up in the midst of a conversation unannounced.

This recently happened to me while ministering prophetically to a sister. As I was prophesying to her in regards to the word of the Lord, which came forth in the form of a vision. I was wrapping up, and then, all of the sudden the gift of knowledge goes to work. I saw another vision of her parents holding hands, and then letting go. Then I saw the word "Divorce". I then asked her how her parents were doing. As she began to share, she began to relay what had been going on with her parents confirming what I had just seen in the vision.

The vision did not say they were getting a divorce, or they had a divorce. The parents had for some time experienced marital troubles, and it may have been moving towards that way. I informed the young lady that I did not know what the outcome would be, but the word of wisdom came. It came in such a way that I did not expect. The word of knowledge revealed the fact of the parents' marital troubles not so to expose their troubles, but to deal with the young lady. She had been struggling through the ordeal, and carrying the burden of the matter. The gift came to give her some wisdom needful for her.

Characteristics of the Gift of Knowledge

1 Samuel 9:18-20 helps us to gain insight regarding the characteristics of the gift. There are four that I want to present here.

1. The identification of the subject of the word of knowledge – the donkeys
2. The specific time regarding the subject – 3 days ago
3. Present reality – they are found
4. The accompanying gift, word of wisdom – do not be anxious about them

Remember, the word of knowledge is the revelation of facts: past and/or present. The word of wisdom is specific, directional, and predictive in nature (dealing with the future); it is something required of you to do in relation to the revealed facts.

John 1:47-49

> **Jesus saw Nathanael coming to Him, and said of him, "Behold, an Israelite indeed, in whom there is no deceit!" Nathanael said to Him, "How do You know me?" Jesus answered and said to him, "Before Philip called you, when you were under the fig tree, I saw you." Nathanael answered Him, "Rabbi, You are the Son of God; You are the King of Israel."** (NASB)

Here we find Jesus ministering in the prophetic. In this text there are two revelation gifts in operation. We will cover the other in the next chapter, but the word of knowledge in this text is operating in a unique manner. Jesus says to Nathaniel, "I saw you under the fig tree." The gift of knowledge also works in such a way as likened to being in a place, but not bodily.

To help give some insight to this, look at Luke 4.

> **Then the devil took Him up to a high mountain and showed Him all the kingdoms of the habitable world in a moment of time [in the twinkling of an eye].** (Verse 5, AMP)

This is a powerful thing taking place here. This moment in the wilderness was a highly spiritual interaction between Christ and Satan. In the natural, Christ was in a desert, but truly, He was engaged with Satan in a spiritual altercation in the spirit realm. The word "moment" there in the Greek is key. The Greek word is stigmē (Strong's Concordance #4743), and it is the word for "an instant". This is how the gift of knowledge operates – in an instant. To better help in understanding the operation of the gift is to understand the way revelation comes – like a flash of lightning. Thus, "word" stands for "a flash of revelation". Lightning can strike once, or it can flash several times. So, the word of knowledge may come in an instant, or even several instances.

Sometimes the word of knowledge operates as if it transports you. Christ was nowhere near Nathaniel, but He saw him. In the Luke four passage, in a moment, Christ is shown the kingdoms of the world. How? It was by way of revelation. This is how He saw Nathaniel, and the nations.

I have experienced this while ministering prophetically to a mother in a church service. As I laid my hand upon her, it was as if I was transported to her neighborhood and then her street. I then was given knowledge of a shooting that had recently taken place, and it was confirmed by those who were with her. She couldn't speak, because she was overcome in relation to receiving the word of the Lord. The accuracy of the word revealed things about her concerns for her children in light of the reality of her neighborhood. Then the first accompanying gift being the discerning of spirits came forth, and then the second accompanying gift being the word of wisdom as well. The collaboration of these gifts revealed to her that God was aware of her concerns for her children and fears, and they addressed God's provision for her in light of the presence of angels about her children. It also gave her what she needed to do – to cease from worrying, and be at rest.

John 4:15-19

> **"Sir," the woman said to Him, "give me this water so I won't get thirsty and come here to draw water." "Go call your husband," He told her, "and come back here." "Go call your husband," He told her, "and come back here." "I don't have a husband," she answered. "You have correctly said, 'I don't have a husband,'" Jesus said. "For you've had five husbands, and the man you now have is not your husband. What you have said is true." "Sir," the woman replied, "I see that You are a prophet." (HCSB)**

Christ is ministering to the Samaritan woman at the well. What's so interesting about this is that this is a very familiar passage on evangelism. Therefore, the gifts are not limited to their expression unto believers, but to unbelievers as well (1 Corinthians 14:24-25). In regards to prophetic evangelism, I recommend the reader to read Sean Evans' book entitled *Prophetic Evangelism*.

The conversation gets to a point where the woman wants this water that Christ is offering her, but He does not present to her an easy way of obtaining it. He gives her the biblical response of repentance and faith in a particular manner, and it is through the word of knowledge. He reveals present and past facts regarding her life and manner of living. She was taken aback, and stated something noteworthy – "I see that You are a prophet." Thus, it is confirmed here that the word of knowledge is a prophetic gift.

The use of the gift did three main things:

1. It revealed the present condition of the woman.
2. It revealed what true repentance would mean for her.

3. It revealed the true identity of Christ; it glorified, magnified, or amplified Christ to her.

John 11:11-15

> **He said this, and then He told them, "Our friend Lazarus has fallen asleep, but I'm on My way to wake him up." Then the disciples said to Him, "Lord, if he has fallen asleep, he will get well." Jesus, however, was speaking about his death, but they thought He was speaking about natural sleep. So Jesus then told them plainly, "Lazarus has died. I'm glad for you that I wasn't there so that you may believe. But let's go to him." (HCSB)**

Christ was informed by those who were sent by the sisters of Lazarus in relation to his condition. He was sick. After some time, Christ turns to His disciples and reveals Lazarus had died. How did He know that? The text does not make mention of any other servants being sent to Him reporting his death. Thus, this is the operation of the word of knowledge.

The word of knowledge helped Christ in regards to timing, because He said that this sickness was not unto death, and that this was for the glory of God. Well, Lazarus died. What glory would God get from this? Then, He stays in the same place for three days. The gift reveals the death of Lazarus, and He determines that it was time to return. At times when this gift comes into play, it will help inform you of the timing to act.

This happens at times while ministering healing to a crowd. Many times ministers would tarry for the Holy Spirit's moving. They would know when He was doing something, because He would begin to reveal present facts of those within the place of various conditions and situations.

Many a times, this is how I would function. I would lead the people in praise and worship. Then I would tarry, pace back and forth, waiting for the Holy Spirit to show me what to do. It would seem that I didn't know what to do, and mostly that would be an accurate assessment. If the Holy Spirit does not do anything, I cannot do anything. However, He is faithful and purposeful. He will manifest Himself through the gifts if we are faithful to wait. The words of Christ sets the precedence – "tarry...till...go" (Luke 24:49, Mark 16:15). We must wait till the Holy Spirit moves.

In those times of ministry, while waiting, He will give me a word of knowledge of a situation or a present fact. It may be someone with a malady, or He will give me a vision of someone or people.

Whatever it is, it is simply to reveal two things:

1. He is present to do something
2. He will do that thing He is present for

When this gift begins to operate, it builds my faith to believe God for whatever He is up to do. It also helps the faith of those who are the recipients of such ministry. Great and exciting things happen when the gifts begin to operate!

Acts 10:17-20

> **While Peter was deeply perplexed about what the vision he had seen might mean, the men who had been sent by Cornelius, having asked directions to Simon's house, stood at the gate. They called out, asking if Simon, who was also named Peter, was lodging there. While Peter was thinking about the vision, the Spirit**

told him, "Three men are here looking for you. Get up, go downstairs, and accompany them with no doubts at all, because I have sent them." (HCSB)

Peter has just received a vision from the Lord Jesus. The vision is confronting his cultural prejudice, and he is trying to reconcile the conflicting thoughts he is having within himself. As he is pondering and revolving the vision within his mind, the gift of knowledge begins to operate. The Holy Spirit says to him "Three men are here looking for you." Peter is upstairs on the roof, but the men are downstairs. How did he know they were in the house? He hadn't been looking down below, for he was in a time of prayer experiencing a vision. The gift of knowledge revealed to him they were there. The gift of wisdom, you can say, also was in operation, for the Holy Spirit directs him to go down to the men, and to go with them without hesitation. Why without hesitation? His cultural prejudice would hinder him from obeying God in light of going to a Gentile's home. Peter was about to come face to face with the meaning of the vision in the latter verses.

This gift, as well as the other gifts, will cause you to rethink things about how God views people. Many a times, you are led to minister to a person who others perceive as being unworthy of God's blessings only to see Him bless the individual. We have our own religious prejudices, traditional hang-ups, and hypocritical facades, but God does not. Neither do the gifts. The gifts are for the profit of all!

The gifts have another function that many do not perceive – sanctification. The more the Holy Spirit works in you, the more you become aware of God's immense love for humanity. You become aware of His power to love all kinds and types of people. The more exposure you get of the gifts, the more you are forced to humbly rid yourself of all types of carnal and fleshly things in you that have no place or right to be there. The gifts will force you to look at yourself, and have you kneeling in repentance simply because God is bigger than our cultural, ethnical, economical, societal, and religious hang-ups.

How can someone be used of God, and have such prejudices? Remember, these gifts are grace gifts. They are not based upon the merit of the believer, but the goodness of the Giver. Peter goes to the house of Cornelius, and says a powerful thing – **"In truth I perceive that God shows no partiality. But in every nation whoever fears Him and works righteousness is accepted by Him."** (Acts 10:34-35, NKJV) This was a big step for Peter, and it will be a big step for us in operating in the gifts of the Spirit.

In the next chapter, I will deal with the next gift being the discerning of spirits.

SUMMARY

The word of knowledge is:

1. A portion of His knowledge from the storehouse of His essence.
2. Always a brief summation of a past or present fact(s).
3. An inward working of the Holy Spirit within a Spirit-filled believer.
4. A leading gift; It is mostly a gift that is accompanied by other gifts in order for it to be of benefit to another person.
5. A gift which imparts and/or activates faith in God.
6. A gift which comes in an instant.
7. A sanctifying gift as all the others.

Chapter 5

The Supernatural Gift of Discerning(s) of Spirits

"To another discerning of spirits [by the same Spirit]..." (1 Corinthians 12:10, NKJV)

We come to the last gift of this first grouping – discerning of spirits. The discerning of spirits is an interesting gift. First of all, this particular gift primarily does not always stand alone. It is a gift that usually has assistance for it to be relevant. Like the word of knowledge, it is a lead gift. It gives way for the expression of another gift(s).

This gift is also listed interestingly. In the original language, it is in the plural – "discernings of spirits". In relation to "spirits", this means that this gift has the ability to distinguish between various types or classes of spirits. "Discernings" is unique as well in the sense that the way of revelation is varied. This gift does not operate in one way, but in multiple and varied ways. This is critical to understand.

To help gain some insight into this is to understand the **anointing**. To "anoint" someone means that they are smeared with oil according to the New Testament as noted in James five verse fourteen. The understanding of to "anoint" in the Old Testament means "to pour". This is captured in Psalms.

Psalms 133:1-3

> **How wonderful and pleasant it is when brothers live together in harmony! For harmony is as precious as the anointing oil that was poured over Aaron's head, that ran down his beard and onto the border of his robe. Harmony is as refreshing as the dew from Mount Hermon that falls on the mountains of Zion. And there the LORD has pronounced his blessing, even life everlasting.** (NLT)

When someone was anointed, the oil was poured out from a container upon the head of the recipient whereby they were covered from head to toe in regards to the oil. So, to be "anointed" meant your whole body was consecrated to the use of God. It spoke even above that in the New Testament. Not only was the whole body consecrated, but the whole personality of man (i.e., spirit, soul, and body) was consecrated.

The gift of the discerning of spirits operates at times in the use of the other aspects of one's personality. The revelation may come by way of your:

- Spirit (i.e., your knower) – the part of you that just knows that there is a spirit present. You don't know how you know, except you just know. This knowing comes by way of revelation to your spirit by the operation of the Spirit of God.
- Soul – a feeling or sense (i.e., the sense of the spirit of fear, or reverence [in response to the presence of God]), or a thought that is brought about by the activity of the Spirit of

God, which enables you to relate to spirits in the supernatural realm.

- Body – physical sensations, such as the natural sensation of smell. My wife has been privileged to have caught the scent of our Lord. Another person may experience the natural sense of sight where you may literally see the presence of a spirit, or it may be the identification of the operation of an evil spirit as in the form of a dark shadow.

When we speak in regards to spirits, we are not referencing one class of spirits. There are different classes of spirits as listed in the following list.

Different Classes of Spirits:

1. Divine – John 4:24
2. Human – 1 Thessalonians 5:19
3. Angelic – Hebrews 1:14
4. Demonic – Revelation 16:14
5. Spiritual realities – 2 Corinthians 4:13

Let's give an example for each of these classes.

Divine

Let us first establish something right off the bat with this one.

John 1:18

> **No one has ever seen God. The One and Only Son – the One who is at the Father's side – He has revealed Him.** (HCSB)

1 Timothy 6:16

> **He alone can never die, and he lives in light so brilliant that no human can approach him. No human eye has ever seen him, nor ever will. All honor and power to him forever! Amen.** (NLT)

1 John 4:12a

> **No one has seen God at any time.** (NKJV)

These portions of Scripture reveal a powerful truth: no one has ever seen God in His literal spiritual form, except the Only Begotten of the Father (Jesus, the Son of God; I would also add the Holy Spirit) who has declared Him.

What about the references we have in Scripture of men having seen God? It was the operation of the gift of the discerning of spirits.

Exodus 33:18-23

> **Then Moses said, "Please, let me see Your glory." He said, "I will cause all My goodness to pass in front of you, and I will proclaim the name Yahweh before you. I will be gracious to whom I will be gracious, and I will have compassion on whom I will have compassion." But He answered, "You cannot see My face, for no one can see Me and live." The LORD said, "Here is a place near Me. You are to stand on the rock, and when My glory passes by, I will put you in the crevice of the rock and cover you with My hand until I have passed by. Then I will take My hand away, and you will see My back, but My face will not be seen." (NKJV)**

This actually happens in the following chapter. What I want to highlight is the last part of His statement to Moses, "You will see My back." God is a spirit, so how would he have seen God's back? The discerning of spirits enables you to see God in ways palatable to the human conscience and personality in which it registers, so man can relate accordingly to God. It is what we find in the phrase – God presented in a natural and/or humanistic way. The theological term is "theophany".

Let's look at a New Testament text to this gift in operation.

Matthew 3:16, 17

> **As soon as Jesus was baptized, he went up out of the water. At that moment heaven was opened, and he saw the Spirit of God descending like a dove and alighting on him. And a voice from heaven said, "This is my Son, whom I love; with him I am well pleased." (NIV)**

In this example, we see the gift in operation in this sense – it discerns that the dove in fact is the Holy Spirit. The key word to hone in on is the word "like". The Holy Spirit is not literally a dove, but the gift presented the Spirit as likened to a dove. There is much symbolism here as to why a dove:

- Peace – the Holy Spirit is the seal of our peace with God, and is the administrator of peace from God.
- Purity – the Holy Spirit purifies or sanctifies us to be like Christ.
- Gentleness – the Holy Spirit gently guides us, and matures us.
- Gracefulness – the Holy Spirit imparts to us the grace of God for living and for service.

Human

John 1:47-48

> **Then Jesus saw Nathanael coming toward Him and said about him, "Here is a true Israelite; no deceit is in him." "How do you know me?" Nathanael asked. "Before Philip called you, when you were under the fig tree, I saw you," Jesus answered.** (HCSB)

Jesus did not just see the physical Nathaniel coming, but He saw his spirit. What I mean specifically and contextually is that Christ saw the true nature or heart of Nathaniel. The discerning of spirits enables you to see past the outward and natural man, and to see the true state or spiritual character of a person (1 Samuel 16:6-7).

Acts 8:18-23

> **When Simon saw that the Holy Spirit was given through the laying on of the apostles' hands, he offered them money, saying, "Give me this power too, so that anyone I lay hands on may receive the Holy Spirit." But Peter told him, "May your silver be destroyed with you, because you thought the gift of God could be obtained with money! You have no part or share in this matter, because your heart is not right before God. Therefore repent of this wickedness of yours, and pray to the Lord that the intent of your heart may be forgiven you. For I see (i.e., discern) you are poisoned by bitterness and bound by iniquity."** (HCSB)

Peter saw right through the guise of Simon by the gift of the discerning of spirits. Simon wanted to reclaim his old status, and he thought what he would need to do is gain the secret by paying for the knowledge. That was the custom of his day, but the Holy Spirit cannot be bought! He has to be received by having been born again first, and then by faith in the reality of the baptism.

Angelic

Daniel 6:19-22

> **At the first light of dawn the king got up and hurried to the lions' den. When he reached the den, he cried out in anguish to Daniel. "Daniel, servant of the living God," the king said, "has your God whom you serve continually been able to rescue you from the lions?" Then Daniel spoke with the king: "May the king live forever. My God sent His angel and shut the lions' mouths. They haven't hurt me, for I was found innocent before Him. Also, I have not committed a crime against you my king." (NKJV)**

How did Daniel know an angel was sent to shut the mouths of the lions (i.e., took away or suspended their appetite for the time being)? It was the gift of discerning of spirits.

Genesis 28:10-12

> **Now Jacob went out from Beersheba and went toward Haran. So he came to a certain place and stayed there all night, because the sun had set. And he took one of the stones of that place and put it at his head, and he lay down in that place to sleep. Then he dreamed, and**

behold, a ladder was set up on the earth, and its top reached to heaven; and there the angels of God were ascending and descending on it. (NKJV)

Here we see that Jacob is sleeping, and he has a dream. In the dream, he sees angels going up and down between heaven and earth. The gift of discerning of spirits is operating in the form of a dream. There's another incident in which Jacob physically encounters angels.

Genesis 32:1, 2

Jacob went on his way, and God's angels met him. When he saw them, Jacob said, "This is God's camp." So he called that place Mahanaim. (NKJV)

The text simply states, **"God's angels met him"**. How did Jacob know that they were angels? The gift revealed it to him. It was a revelation to his spirit; it was an inward knowing.

Also, notice this portion of Scripture, **"Don't neglect to show hospitality, for by doing this some have welcomed angels as guests without knowing it."** (Hebrews 13:2, HCSB) The point of the text is to always be hospitable to strangers, because you never know that you could be entertaining an angel. This has been the case for many people who have had encounters with angels. But for those who knew it was an angel they had encountered, how did they know? By this gift! This gift was in operation to help them interact with the spirit sent from God. You will not always know it is an angel; however, there are times you will know by virtue of the Holy Spirit through the operation of this gift.

Demonic

1 Kings 22:1-23

Due to the length of the reference, please take this moment to read the passage before moving on in the chapter.

In this real yet comical passage, we find a lying spirit allowed to go and deceive the kings through the prophets gathered before them. What seems to be genuinely outward is actually the operation of a demonic spirit seeking to deceive. We must be careful to test the spirits to ascertain the genuine source of the prophetic utterance. One of the ways to discern is by the gift of discerning of spirits.

Acts 16:16-18

> **Now it happened, as we went to prayer, that a certain slave girl possessed with a spirit of divination met us, who brought her masters much profit by fortune-telling. This girl followed Paul and us, and cried out, saying, "These men are the servants of the Most High God, who proclaim to us the way of salvation." And this she did for many days. But Paul, greatly annoyed, turned and said to the spirit, "I command you in the name of Jesus Christ to come out of her." And he came out that very hour.** (NKJV)

Here, we find the apostle being confronted by a slave girl who has a demonic spirit that enabled her to practice divination. The Greek word pneuma (English, spirit), which is used to refer to the Spirit of God, is also the same word used to speak of this demonic spirit. The next Greek word is the word pythōn, which is identified as "in Greek mythology the name of the Pythian serpent or dragon that dwelt in the region of Pytho at the foot of Parnassus in Phocis, and was said to have guarded the oracle at Delphi and been slain by Apollo." (Thayer's Greek Lexicon)

This spirit, likened to a serpent or dragon god, is the spirit by which this slave girl operated in to predict things. Furthermore, a python, in the animal kingdom, is a boa constrictor, which is a large non-venomous serpent that kills by coiling around its prey, and according to current studies, kills its prey by circulatory arrest.[1] This means that the blood of its prey ceases to flow. This is the nature of this spirit – to deprive the activity of authentic Holy Spirit ministry in relation to the blood of Christ. The spirit tried to present itself either on equal footing with the Spirit, or tries to mask itself as the true Holy Spirit.

This is the challenge that we face in the Church today – how to discern an actual spirit behind an utterance. This gift is an invaluable resource within the body of Christ. We must allow those with this gift the freedom to express it. For in doing so, they will bring about safety and protection to the flock of Christ.

Spiritual Realities

Acts 14:8-10

In Lystra a man without strength in his feet, lame from birth, and who had never walked, sat and heard Paul speaking. After observing him closely and seeing that he had faith to be healed, Paul said in a loud

---

[1] Geggel, Laura. **Not by Suffocation: Study Unveils the Real Way Boa Constrictors Kill**. Live Science, 7/23/15. Cite: http://www.nbcnews.com/science/weird-science/not-suffocation-study-unveils-real-way-boa-constrictors-kill-n397471?cid=sm_fb

voice, "Stand upright on your feet!" And he jumped up and started to walk around. (NKJV)

Paul, by the operation of the discerning of spirits, saw (i.e., discerned) the crippled man had faith to be healed. What did he see? Paul saw his faith. Faith is a spiritual reality, and can be seen by the discerning of spirits.

At this point, let me share what I have experienced regarding this gift of the discerning of spirits. In my ministry, I have sensed, seen, and heard angelic spirits. I have not seen an angel in the presentation of a human form (Hebrews 13:2), but I have experienced them in the sense of a closed vision.

The gift of the discerning of spirits has operated in ways to angels differently for me, but are not limited to this list:

- I have seen them in shaded color
- As body guards, like secret service men (in a closed vision)
- Likened to a roman soldier coming to me in a dream

In relation to demonic spirits:

- I have heard demons growl
- I have sensed their presence
- My wife has picked up their scent
- Discerned their presence, and once I mentioned their presence, they would take the person and throw them down to the ground.
- Picked up their presence in an atmosphere (i.e., an environment or locale – over a local assembly, neighborhood, community, or region)

- Seen the spirit of depression as likened to a dark fog over the head of a person, or have seen the presence of the spirit of depression upon the face of a person

In relation to God:

- I have seen the hand of God
- The presence of God
- The wind of the Spirit blowing

I have come to find out what the wind of the Spirit blowing means (to me), and it can be found in the following verses.

John 3:7-8

> **So don't be so surprised when I tell you that you have to be "born from above"—out of this world, so to speak. You know well enough how the wind blows this way and that. You hear it rustling through the trees, but you have no idea where it comes from or where it's headed next. That's the way it is with everyone "born from above" by the wind of God, the Spirit of God.** (MSG)

Revelation 2:7

> **Are your ears awake? Listen. Listen to the Wind Words, the Spirit blowing through the churches...** (MSG)

In the next chapter, we will cover the supernatural gift of faith.

SUMMARY

The gift of discerning of spirits:

1. Operates at times in the use of the other aspects of one's personality (spirit, soul, and body).
2. Enables you to see spirits in ways palatable to the human conscience and personality in which it registers whereby one can relate accordingly to that spirit.
3. Enables one to see past the outer & natural man, and to see the true state or character of the person.
4. Is a means of testing the spirits to ascertain the genuine source of prophetic utterance, and/or supernatural activity.

Chapter 6

The Supernatural Gift of Faith

To another faith by the same Spirit... (1 Corinthians 12:9, NKJV)

Last chapter, we covered the first grouping – the revelation gifts:

1. Word of wisdom
2. Word of knowledge
3. Discerning of spirits

Now we are moving into the next grouping which is the power gifts:

1. Gift of faith
2. Gifts of healings
3. Working of miracles

We are going to be dealing with the first of this section being the gift of faith. In order to make the distinction between the "gift of faith" versus "faith", we are going to look at the various facets of faith.

The Greek word for faith is pistis (Strong's Concordance #4102), which is defined as "the conviction of the truth of anything. In the New Testament, it speaks of a conviction or belief respecting man's relationship to God and divine things." (Thayer's Lexicon) This Greek word is used predominantly for faith in the New Testament. I define faith as **conviction in God's identity and confidence in God's ability**.

Let's take a look at how faith is described in the Bible.

Saving Faith (Ephesians 2:8-9, James 2:14, Romans 10:17)

This is the faith which one receives at the time of conversion. Salvation is truly the work of the Spirit within the human heart. One cannot even believe apart from the influence of the Spirit, for:

- the consciousness of man is seared (1 Timothy 4:2)
- his intellect is darkened (2 Corinthians 4:4)
- his spirit is dead (Ephesians 2:1)

Therefore, the Holy Spirit is the One that convinces the mind and convicts the heart regarding sin, judgment, and righteousness (John 16:8; Acts 2:37). This initial faith is the faith that serves as the conduit for God's grace to save.

Measure of Faith (Romans 12:3)

This "measure of faith" speaks to the deposit of saving faith, which now becomes a permanent reality within the heart of man. For each person who has received this faith, it is different in its amount. Why? I am not sure, but I could conjecture that it is in relation to each person's spiritual matrix. Each person's reality prior to conversion is quite different, and requires a certain measure to believe God. How gracious is our God!

Maturing Faith (Galatians 5:22, 2 Thessalonians 1:3, c.f., James 1:3)

This measure can be increased or matured through a process. The process is found in James – the trying of our faith through various trials. Faith here then is likened to a muscle that can be built up, or it can atrophy, which means that your faith gradually fails in effectiveness or strength due to underuse or negligence. Your faith was not merely given to you to be saved, but to be used far beyond the point of conversion.

Gift of Faith (1 Corinthians 12:9, Mark 11:22)

The gift of faith is completely different in nature. The first three speak to the fact of faith given by God for **salvation**, and for Christian **daily living** and **daily service**. I relate to them as "spiritual human faith". The gift of faith, however, is "supernatural divine faith". It is a supernatural gift that operates just like the other nine gifts listed within this portion of Scripture. **This gift of faith is a temporary operation or manifestation of the Spirit within a believer for the purpose of manifesting a supernatural feat beyond man's own matured measure of faith**. It is a faith that comes into play in a moment to produce a powerful and dramatic display of God's power.

This faith does not come through constant meditation, but by the operation of the Spirit. You cannot hype this gift up. It is a voluntary sovereign work of the Spirit within the heart of a Spirit-filled believer when the need arises. Another way of seeing this faith is to see it as the faith of God **temporarily imparted** unto a Spirit-filled believer.

Faith is a needful ingredient in regards to the gifts. Therefore, this gift is listed at the top of this grouping. The reason for this is because this gift many a times leads out in ministering instant healings and performing miracles.

Let us take a look at various references in relation to this gift that will help us gain insight into its operation and powerful purpose.

2 Kings 2:19-22

> **Then the men of the city said to Elisha, "Please notice, the situation of this city is pleasant, as my lord sees; but the water is bad, and the ground barren." And he said, "Bring me a new bowl, and put salt in it." So they brought it to him. Then he went out to the source of the water, and cast in the salt there, and said, "Thus says the Lord: 'I have healed this water; from it there shall be no more death or barrenness.' " So the water remains healed to this day, according to the word of Elisha which he spoke.** (NKJV)

Here we find an Old Testament passage for the gift of faith in operation. This is an Old Testament version of the gift. The prophet Elisha heals water by casting salt into the water. He knew this would happen by the gift of faith that came to him as a word.

2 Kings 4:40-44

> **The stew was poured out for the men, but as they began to eat it, they cried out, "Man of God, there is death in the pot!" And they could not eat it. Elisha said, "Get some flour." He put it into the pot and said, "Serve it to the people to eat." And there was nothing harmful in the pot. A man came from Baal Shalishah,**

bringing the man of God twenty loaves of barley
bread baked from the first ripe grain, along with
some heads of new grain. "Give it to the people to
eat," Elisha said. "How can I set this before a hundred
men?" his servant asked. But Elisha answered, "Give
it to the people to eat. For this is what the LORD says:
'They will eat and have some left over.'" Then he set
it before them, and they ate and had some left over,
according to the word of the LORD. (NIV)

Again, we have two references regarding the gift of faith in
the ministry of the prophet Elisha. How did he know the miracles
would occur? The answer is found in what is noted in verse 44 –
"according to the word of the LORD".

Mark 11:12-14, 20-24

The next day when they came out from Bethany, He
was hungry. After seeing in the distance a fig tree
with leaves, He went to find out if there was anything
on it. When He came to it, He found nothing but
leaves, because it was not the season for figs. He said
to it, "May no one ever eat fruit from you again!"
And His disciples heard it.... Early in the morning, as
they were passing by, they saw the fig tree withered
from the roots up. Then Peter remembered and said
to Him, "Rabbi, look! The fig tree that You cursed
is withered." Jesus replied to them, "Have faith in
God. I assure you: If anyone says to this mountain,
'Be lifted up and thrown into the sea,' and does not
doubt in his heart, but believes that what he says will

happen, it will be done for him. Therefore I tell you, all the things you pray and ask for—believe that you have received them, and you will have them. (HCSB)

This article "in" is significant, and in light of the context of the passage, the Greek article is better put as "of". Therefore, Christ here admonishes the disciples to have the faith of God, or have God's faith.

The gift of faith deals with performing feats that are challenges beyond any natural means. This gift is a mountain removing-fig tree withering gift! Christ shows us here within this account of the fig tree, and also the parabolic example of the mountain being removed and cast into the sea, by connecting it with "says to". He also ends the discourse with prayer – "all the things you pray and ask for". Therefore, there are two ways this gift operates: **speaking to** (a declarative word) & **speaking for** (intercession).

This gift also operates through the gift of prophecy. This gift of faith is a portion of the All-Encompassing-Faith of God. Thus, when God spoke creation into existence, it was His faith in His own ability being expressed. This is not strange to understand. When God swore to Abraham, He could not find anyone higher to swear by, so He swore by Himself. He has faith in Himself, and so a declarative word uttered by God is a word of great power. Thus, when He spoke **"Let there be"**, it simply came into existence. Therefore, when we speak a word of faith by the operation of the gift of faith, we can expect to see the same results that God would get if He spoke it directly Himself.

Matthew 14:22-27

Immediately He made the disciples get into the boat and go ahead of Him to the other side, while He dismissed the crowds. After dismissing the crowds,

He went up on the mountain by Himself to pray. When evening came, He was there alone. But the boat was already over a mile from land, battered by the waves, because the wind was against them. Around three in the morning, He came toward them walking on the sea. When the disciples saw Him walking on the sea, they were terrified. "It's a ghost!" they said, and cried out in fear. Immediately Jesus spoke to them. "Have courage! It is I. Don't be afraid." (HCSB)

Here's a classic depiction of the gift in operation. It is not related to healing or deliverance from a demonic presence, but to a natural storm. Notice how the disciples are out on the water in the midst of a storm that has the potential of claiming all of their lives. Christ is at shore praying, and He then goes out walking on the water. Why the delay? Why spend time in prayer?

> Prayer is the earnest request for the intervention & involvement of God in the affairs of men and the cosmos.

We ought to learn from this account of the operation of the gift. It is not a faith that is operational as if on all the time at one's own will. It comes into play at the will of the Holy Spirit. It is given at the moment needed for whatever the insurmountable challenge one may be faced with. In this passage, the challenge was coming to the rescue of the disciples. When Christ entered the boat, the storm stop raging.

One key note, prayer is an important aspect to this gift. Prayer is the earnest request for the intervention & involvement of God in the affairs of men and the cosmos. God can influence men and the universe to accomplish His purposes and for His glory. As we pray (in spiritual human faith), then God will respond by granting us His supernatural divine faith to grant us the ability of performing the supernatural feat.

Another thing to note is that this gift of faith comes into play when our spiritual human faith cannot go where needed; our faith simply isn't enough (Romans 12:3). Therefore, this supernatural gift kicks in like cylinders in a car. If you have a six cylinder car, what usually operates for the car to drive regularly are the 4 cylinders. The two cylinders that sit idly by do so because there is no present pressing need for their operation. The car still moves and accomplishes its task of transportation. However, that changes when the car tries to go up a steep hill; the two idle cylinders suspend their inactivity, and come alive. The two cylinders kick in, and enable the car to reach its final destination, at its appointed mark. That is how the gift works. It is a "kick in" type of gift. It "kicks in" when it is needed.

Those who operate in this sort of gift regularly are those who operate in the ministry of healing, miracles, and deliverance. This gift is needed, because they are faced regularly with situations that are beyond spiritual human faith. It takes the faith of God to move various mountains (1 Corinthians 13:2).

John 2:6-11

> **Now six stone water jars had been set there for Jewish purification. Each contained 20 or 30 gallons. "Fill the jars with water," Jesus told them. So they filled them to the brim. Then He said to them, "Now draw some out and take it to the chief servant." And they did. When the chief servant tasted the water (after it had become wine), he did not know where it came from—though the servants who had drawn the water knew. He called the groom and told him, "Everyone**

sets out the fine wine first, then, after people have drunk freely, the inferior. But you have kept the fine wine until now." Jesus performed this first sign in Cana of Galilee. He displayed His glory, and His disciples believed in Him. (HCSB)

Here is another reference to the operation of the gift of faith. Jesus is at a wedding, and the host of the festivities runs out of wine. Mary, Jesus' mother, turns to Him to make request for His assistance. There seems to have been some resistance on the part of Christ due to timing, but He obliges the request. He calls for the attendants to get water pots, fill them to the brim, and then serve the people wine. What? It is water! Christ, by the gift of faith, knew that the water would be turned into wine by God's power. It was such a miracle that the people who attended the wedding noticed the water which was turned into wine was better than what was served before. Now that is a miracle within itself, because these are people who have been drinking wine for some time, and they were able to differentiate the difference.

The point I want to stress here in regards to this reference is the **dogged unabated faith** of Christ. He did not flinch or was doubtful at all. There was no hesitancy or delay in His behavior regarding the miracle. **The gift of faith has no doubt in it at all. It is a faith that is pervasive and predominant within the heart and mind of an individual at the moment it is activated**. It is a faith that superimposes itself over one's faith. It is recognizably different from one's spiritual human faith. One's faith is likened to the demoniac's father – **"Lord, I believe; help my unbelief!"** (Mark 9:24, NKJV)

59

Spiritual human faith is different than the gift of faith in that it is challenged by unbelief (more specifically in this passage, the word properly translated is "doubt"). However, the gift of faith has no doubt that hinders its effectiveness. Spiritual human faith overcomes doubt by constantly dwelling upon the Word of God (Romans 10:17). The gift of faith, however, comes instantly and operates without any contest (Mark 11:23).

Matthew 14:19-21

> **Then He commanded the multitudes to sit down on the grass. And He took the five loaves and the two fish, and looking up to heaven, He blessed and broke and gave the loaves to the disciples; and the disciples gave to the multitudes. So they all ate and were filled, and they took up twelve baskets full of the fragments that remained. Now those who had eaten were about five thousand men, besides women and children.** (NKJV)

Here again we find this gift in operation in the life and ministry of Christ. Here it is feeding over 5000 people at once. It is the miracle of multiplication. I have heard of this type of miracle taking place on the mission fields on more than one occasion. Again, this miracle is likened to the miracle of water turning into wine. Furthermore, we have a similar occurrence of this type of miracle in the Old Testament by the prophet Elisha (2 Kings 4:42-44).

As you look carefully, all these references are miracles. The multiplication of food, healing of natural water, and the changing of water into wine, they all are miracles. You would think this would be the workings of miracles, and you would be correct. However, these manifestations occur in conjunction with the gift of faith. As mentioned before, the gift is a leading gift. It leads out the other power gifts many a times due to the nature of the feat before a Spirit-filled believer. The gift of faith takes up where your spiritual human faith leaves off.

In the next chapter, we are going to look at the next gift being the gifts of healings. We will come to see this powerful gift in operation.

SUMMARY

The gift of faith is:

1. "Supernatural divine faith".
2. A portion of the all-encompassing-faith of God.
3. A temporary operation or manifestation of the Spirit within a believer for the purpose of manifesting a supernatural feat beyond man's own matured measure of faith stemming back to the point of conversion.
4. A faith that has no doubt in it at all. It is a faith that is pervasive and predominant within the heart and mind of an individual at the moment it is activated. It is a faith that superimposes itself over one's spiritual human faith.
5. A faith that will cause things to come into being or reality supernaturally.
6. Faith that comes into play at the will of the Holy Spirit. It is given at the moment needed to produce a powerful and dramatic display of God's power for whatever the insurmountable challenge one may be faced with.
7. Faith that takes up where your spiritual human faith leaves off.

Chapter 7

The Gifts of Healings

To another gifts of healings by the same Spirit... (1 Corinthians 12:9, NKJV)

As we continue in this study, we come to the gifts of healings. Let us move to defining the gift. Again, notice how the gift is put forth by the apostle – gifts of healings. In the original language, both "gifts" and "healings" are in the plural form. This is like what we saw with the gift of the discerning of spirits.

Let us look at the first word of this gift. When Paul relates to "gifts", he is stating two things:

1.   Healing is a gift from God to a person who is sick. A person does not earn healing from God, but it is an act of God's mercy, goodness, and grace.

Luke 11:11-13

What father among you, if his son asks for a loaf of bread, will give him a stone; or if he asks for a fish,

will instead of a fish give him a serpent? Or if he asks for an egg, will give him a scorpion? If you then, evil as you are, know how to give good gifts [gifts that are to their advantage] to your children, how much more will your heavenly Father give the Holy Spirit to those who ask and continue to ask Him! (AMP)

2. Healing comes or is administered in various ways.

Job 5:9

Who does great things, and unsearchable, marvelous things without number? (KJV)

Job 9:10

He does great things past finding out, yes, wonders without number. (NKJV)

Romans 11:33

Oh, the depth of the riches both of the wisdom and knowledge of God! How unsearchable are His judgments and unfathomable His ways! (NASB)

If you notice the ministry of Jesus, you will see that He usually ministers healing in different ways. To give a biblical example of this, let us look at the example of Christ having ministered to those who were blind:

a. Mark 8:22-26

Then they came to Bethsaida. They brought a blind man to Him and begged Him to touch him. He took the blind man by the hand and brought him out of the village. Spitting on his eyes and laying His hands on him, He asked him, "Do you see anything?" He looked up and said, "I see people—they look to me like trees walking." Again Jesus placed His hands on the man's eyes, and he saw distinctly. He was cured and could see everything clearly. Then He sent him home, saying, "Don't even go into the village." (HCSB)

Here Jesus touched the eyes of the blind man. This would be an example of the laying on of hands.

b. Mark 10:51-52

Then Jesus answered him, "What do you want Me to do for you?" "Rabbouni," the blind man told Him, "I want to see!" "Go your way," Jesus told him. "Your faith has healed you." Immediately he could see and began to follow Him on the road. (HCSB)

Jesus did not touch blind Bartimaeus. He simply gave him the command, "Go your way."

c. John 9:1, 6-7

As He was passing by, He saw a man blind from birth. After He said these things He spit on the ground, made some mud from the saliva, and spread the mud on his eyes. "Go," He told him, "wash in the pool of Siloam" (which means "Sent"). So he left, washed, and came back seeing. (HCSB)

In the first two examples, Christ laid His hands, and the next He gave a command (i.e., decree, demand, authoritative command). Here, Jesus anointed the man's eyes with mud which He made with His saliva and the dirt of the ground. These three examples shows the diversity of the Spirit. The Spirit is not limited in the ways He determines to bring healing to a person. There are many more ways the Spirit can lead a person to administer healing, but we must be opened to His leading. This is the very nature of what it means to be filled – yielded-ness to the leading of the Spirit.

I, personally, have experienced the various ways the Spirit has worked this gift in my ministry. The predominant way I have experienced this particular gift has been by the laying on of hands. This follows the model presented to us in Scripture (Mark 16:17-18). I have experienced this gift in the manner of making a decree. It has also been administered by blowing upon people. You would wonder why blowing on someone? It represents prophetically what God did in the creation account of man.

Genesis 2:7

> **Then the Lord God formed the man out of the dust from the ground and breathed the breath of life into his nostrils, and the man became a living being.** (HCSB)

Psalms 104:29, 30

> **You hide Your face, they are dismayed; You take away their spirit, they expire and return to their dust. You send forth Your Spirit, they are created; and You renew the face of the ground.** (NASB)

John 20:22

After saying this, He breathed on them and said, "Receive the Holy Spirit." (NKJV)

But I must state, you cannot in and of your own will decide which method will be used to administer healing. That is of the will and decision of the Holy Spirit. The common and predominant method or means given in Scripture, even by our Lord (Mark 16:17-18), is by the laying on of hands. So, if you are not given any specific way to minister healing, default to the common biblical manner – lay hands on the sick, and stand on the promise of God – the sick will recover (Mark 16:17-18, James 5:14-16).

Let us move to the other word translated for our English word "healings". As the first part dealt with the varied ways of ministering healing, "healings" deals with the limitless ability of God to administer healing to various types of sickness. In the ministry of Christ, He faced various types of sicknesses and diseases. There was not a medical disease that He could not heal. Therefore, the gifts of healings brings healing to whatever the malady may be.

We have established the fact that this gift can be administered in various ways to various kinds of illnesses. The next thing I want to address is the fact that this gift causes healing to manifest over a period of time. Simply, healing is gradual. This means that when healing happens, it will not present itself immediately. When a healing happens immediately, it is a miracle.

When operating in the gifts of healings, the Spirit will quicken the mortal body.

Romans 8:10, 11

> **And if Christ be in you, the body is dead because of sin; but the Spirit is life because of righteousness. But if the Spirit of him that raised up Jesus from the dead dwell in you, he that raised up Christ from the dead shall also quicken your mortal bodies by his Spirit that dwelleth in you.** (KJV)

The Old English term used in the King James Version is a great word to choose for the translation for the Greek term zōopoieō (Strong's Concordance #2227). The word means "to reanimate, to restore life, to make alive". Looking at the Old English root, it means "living, alive, lively, and swift". This word here in Romans captures the sense that when the Holy Spirit quickens the mortal (i.e., susceptible to death) body, it not only restores it to life, but a life that is full of vigor and new found vitality.

Isaiah's prophetic words are true here, and let's read it in the Amplified version.

Isaiah 40:28–31

> **Have you not known? Have you not heard? The everlasting God, the Lord, the Creator of the ends of the earth, does not faint or grow weary; there is no searching of His understanding. He gives power to the faint and weary, and to him who has no might He increases strength [causing it to multiply and making it to abound]. Even youths shall faint and be weary, and [selected] young men shall feebly stumble and fall exhausted; But those who wait for the Lord [who expect, look for, and hope in Him] shall change and**

**renew their strength and power; they shall lift their
wings and mount up [close to God] as eagles [mount
up to the sun]; they shall run and not be weary, they
shall walk and not faint or become tired.** (AMP)

There is some other things about this gift and the nature of
healing we need to understand. When healing occurs, it is not only
gradual, but it is progressive. The word progress can be defined as
something which moves towards a goal or a more developed stage; it
carries the understanding of a continuity of increased advancement.
Thus, the gifts of healings interrupts the path of sickness, and
reverses it towards the goal of recovery. Not only that, but God
has increased the strength of the person through the gift. Looking at Isaiah 40:31 again, in the Amplified Version, it states **"He increases strength [causing it to multiply and making it to abound]."** He does not just give strength, but abounding strength. Thus,

> **Healing is:**
>
> - **Gradual**
> - **Progressive**
> - **Imperceptible to the Senses**

when the person has recovered, he or she will have noticed that they
have a vigor they haven't known for years.

Lastly, it is imperceptible. When this gift is in operation, the
recipient of such ministry can miss the fact that they are healed.
This is important, because God has touched a person through faith.
Faith must remain in order for healing to gradually progress to its
expected conclusion. Our doubt through reasoning can short circuit
the healing process, so remain in faith through thanksgiving and
praise (Romans 4:20).

Ephesians 2:8 states, **"For by grace you have been saved
through faith; and that not of yourselves, it is the gift of God."**

(NASB) Grace is God's unmerited favor, but it is also understood as His abounding power (2 Corinthians 12:9). The channel for God's grace is our faith. As we place our faith in Him, He is able to move through this channel to bring about the healing we so desperately seek. As this grace is operating, if we cease to receive it by faith, then we rob ourselves of the finished work of the gift.

Derek Prince many times would tell those at the altar seeking their healing "Stay connected!" The imagery that I get is that of an appliance plugged into an electric socket. The electric socket has volts of electricity flowing unceasingly, and it is untapped until an appliance is connected to the socket by a plug. Once connected, the appliance has tapped into an unceasing supply of power to be used. When the appliance is turned on, the appliance is operational and is able to produce what it was created for. Once disconnected, the power ceases to flow, and so does the operation of the appliance. Consequently, the intended result is never fully realized.

Here is the spiritual understanding of this analogy. The socket is the untapped source of God's ability to produce healing. The appliance represents our faith. As we connect to Him through faith, we are able to experience the boundless and abounding power of His grace to produce healing. His healing power will course through, and heal the body. However, we must remain connected to the source in order to experience the full measure of His healing.

Now, here's the thing. His grace is boundless, but our faith is by measure (Romans 12:3, 6). His measureless grace is coursing through to produce healing by a measured faith. Healing takes time simply because of a boundless reality flowing through a measured means. Stay connected till your healing has been completed, for "He is also able to save to the uttermost those who come to God through Him, since He always lives to make intercession for them." (Hebrews 7:25, NKJV)

The Greek word for uttermost is pantelēs (Strong's Concordance #3838), which means "all complete, perfect"; contextually, it means "unto completeness". (Thayer's Lexicon) God is able to heal a person unto completeness of health. It may take time, but He will do it. When He does, He leaves all men amazed.

Let us look at some examples of this gift in Scripture.

2 Kings 5:1, 9, 10, 14

> **Naaman, commander of the army for the king of Aram, was a great man in his master's sight and highly regarded because through him, the LORD had given victory to Aram. The man was a brave warrior, but he had a skin disease....So Naaman came with his horses and chariots and stood at the door of Elisha's house. Then Elisha sent him a messenger, who said, "Go wash seven times in the Jordan and your flesh will be restored and you will be clean."...So Naaman went down and dipped himself in the Jordan seven times, according to the command of the man of God. Then his skin was restored and became like the skin of a small boy, and he was clean.** (HCSB)

Notice how Naaman had to dip himself seven times in the river. The number "seven" speaks of completion and perfection, for He is able to save to the uttermost as we saw earlier. He is not healed on the first try, nor the second, or even the third. It is when he does so on the seventh dip that Naaman is completely healed. Healing takes time, but if we persist (Luke 18:1, 8), we will experience the complete or finished work of the Spirit.

Remember what I shared about the progressive work of healing? Look at the words of the author here, **"his skin was restored and became like the skin of a small boy..."** That is the nature of healing. He did not only heal Naaman, but restored his skin to such a state as that of a newborn's skin. Again, we will deal with this further in the next chapter at some length.

I must state something here that is of importance. Seeking divine healing requires a certain mentality. We are of the microwave generation. We want everything quick, even when it comes to healing. However, you need to have a mindset where you will not give up till your healing comes or manifests. The psalmist captured this sort of mental fortitude in Psalm 118.

Psalms 118:17

> **I shall not die, but live, and declare the works of the Lord.** (NKJV)

When we understand healing requires persistence, it changes our mindset to press hard after God who is the healer. Christ died to secure the benefit of healing (Psalm 103:3; Isaiah 53:5, 1 Peter 2:24), but as He stated in Matthew, **"From the days of John the Baptist until now, the kingdom of heaven has been suffering violence, and the [persistently] violent have been seizing it by force."** (Matthew 11:12, HCSB) This was the mindset of Christ, and it is how He ministered to the masses of sick people. He would not quit till the person was healed.

Mark 8:22-25

> **Then they came to Bethsaida. They brought a blind man to Him and begged Him to touch him. He took the blind man by the hand and brought him out of**

the village. Spitting on his eyes and laying His hands on him, He asked him, "Do you see anything?" He looked up and said, "I see people—they look to me like trees walking." Again Jesus placed His hands on the man's eyes, and he saw distinctly. He was cured and could see everything clearly. (HCSB)

Notice how the blind man did not gain his sight immediately. He saw, but it was not clear. Christ laid hands on him again, and after that the man was healed; he was able to see clearly. Healing is like that. You have to keep pressing till the full manifestation comes. Stay connected and keep pressing through persistence!

Let me now share from my own experiences with this gift.

1. A Child with Mental Disorder

I remember praying for a child who was considered to be mentally ill, and after a few days, the testimony regarding that child was she was like a different child.

2. A Sister with Back Pain

I remember praying for a sister at an event, and I remember hugging her, and immediately the word of knowledge revealed that she had a back issue. I began to pray, and it was as if I was shown an x-ray vision of her spine and the nerve connections. I began to pray for them to be repaired. After praying for her, she relayed to me that she did not share such knowledge with anyone that she had the issue, and the only way I could have known that was by the Lord. She later told me that her back no longer had the pain.

Now, I would like to share two testimonies of a dear brother and sister in the Lord who were healed. These testimonies make clear the nature of this gift, and give glory to God our healer (Jehovah Rapha').

Mark's Testimony

In 2007, I was diagnosed with hypertension. I refused to believe I had to take the medication all my life as stated by the doctor. I started to take the meds, but then stopped because it wasn't agreeing with me (headaches) and I knew the meds can cause other complications.

In 2008, I rushed to the hospital from work with sharp pain in my chest. The pressure was very high. I remember the top number being 171. The very next day after taking several tests, I went into my doctor's office. My doctor asked was I taking the meds. I told him no, for all of the reasons I mentioned above. The doctor then began to explain to me that I had to take the meds and the urgency/importance. I asked the doctor how long would I have to take the meds, he mentioned all of my life. That didn't sit well with me at all. I was trying to obey my doctor's orders, but it just didn't sit well.

In 2010, Pastor Powell spoke a message on Wednesday Word Explosion (Mid-Week Bible Study) entitled "Prayer Works". Pastor mentioned if we are to believe God, there should be some accompanying works. Pastor also mentioned that many people state they have faith in God, but put their trust in other things. Furthermore, in the message, Pastor mentioned don't wait for the doctor to give us a negative report, but we should start using our faith to believe for healing. The pastor also mentioned years ago many didn't have the luxury of medication as we do now. Those people then used their faith, and were healed.

Later on in 2010, I thought to myself, I really need to fully "trust and believe" that I am healed. I started to walk, meditate, fast, and change my diet (no salt). I then stopped taking the meds once again.

I remember the season was changing, and I had severe headaches. I thought to myself, I wonder if this hypertension thing is trying to distract me, so I went to the pharmacy to check my pressure. It was a Sunday. On the next day there was an evangelism training at Agape set up in the fellowship hall. The title of the training was "Evangelism in Conjunction with Signs and Wonders", specifically emphasizing healing. We formed in groups of 4-5, and the direction was to be lead in prayer, and begin to pray for one another in the group. Well into the prayer, I remember Christina (Elder's wife) & Elder Evans paused everyone in the room, and stated clearly that someone was suffering with a heart issue.

Then all of a sudden my group all laid hands on me and begun to pray. I remember during the prayer, I was telling God "I receive my healing in the name of Jesus". We then paused again, and Elder Evans said the person with the heart issue will go to the doctor and have a praise report. I remember it just like yesterday! He also mentioned that it was going to blow the doctor's mind.

I had set up a doctor's appointment earlier in the day (Monday) prior to the evangelism training. The appointment was for the end of the week. When I arrived at the doctor's office, it was the normal routine. The doctor checked my pressure, went to his records and looked at me, and stated, "The meds are working for you I see." Before I go further, I was seeing the doctor periodically prior to evangelism class and after the Wednesday word explosion. So he was taking my pressure all along. When he stated that he saw that the meds was working for me, I stated, "Doc, to be honest I haven't been taking the meds." He looked up at me, and paused. I said to myself, here we go. He is going to try and sell me this stuff. He asked me, "So, you're not taking the meds?" I said, "Yes sir. I'm not taking the meds." The doctor then stated I do not need them anymore. I thought I didn't hear him correctly so I asked for how long? He said I don't need them anymore.

I jumped out of my seat excited to go tell Elder Dorcas and Elder Evans of my praise report. I reached elder Dorcas as soon as I left the office.

Shalom,
Mark

Kathy's Testimony

There were major changes in my school due to budget cuts and supposedly school reform. While we were in the beginning of the 2012-2013 school year, the principal had to close my special needs classroom to accommodate a Gift and Talented Class. I then noticed that I was protruding and at the news of the changes I began to stress even more which also added to the pain. The weight was also adding up, and the fear of not knowing what was wrong with my body was taking its toll.

I came to school one day, and one of the administrators was in the class with another colleague. She was waiting for me so that she can share Deon Kipping's new album. He visited Agape Family Worship Center that prior weekend. She was playing, "I don't look Like (What I Went Through)". I began to cry, I never did that before, but all of the stress along with just losing my father. She held me while I cried while I was telling her how everything was bothering me, and that I didn't know what was going on with my body. I first heard that song when I was in South Carolina with my mom that past summer. When I heard that song, it brought that pain along with the physical pain I was enduring, so the administrator told me that I was going to church with her that night. I wasn't expecting anything other than prayer or encouragement when I attended.

When I came to the church (evangelism training), I was rather nervous and didn't really want to go, because I wasn't expecting anything. I have a relationship with the Lord, but I still had this sense of fear and anxiety over me. I would always pray for others and see breakthroughs for those who I prayed for, but for myself, there was some breakthroughs, but I felt my faith wasn't strong enough. Elder Pierre asked if there are those with heart burn and acid reflux. I got up for that purpose. We were instructed to raise our hands to give the Lord praise with expectancy. My hands were raised, and when he finally got to me, he asked if I had any problems with my stomach? I told him, "Yes." He told me that we will agree that it's healed, but first go to the doctor to see what's wrong and it will be a gradual healing. After we agreed, and the Elder prayed over my stomach, the pain disappeared.

The following Tuesday is when I went to an assigned OB/GYN and the doctor told me I had a fibroid the size of a cantaloupe. He told me that I would need to have it removed. I told my younger sister of the diagnosis, and she was telling me to get the procedure done, but I was not feeling that in my spirit. That same evening my church has prayer and Bible Study. After Bible Study, I went to my Pastor and we agreed that I will not need surgery. I believe with prayer and agreement with Elder Pierre, it built my faith, and I have seen gradual healing. I still have no pain, my weight and my stomach went down since he prayed over me. Thank the Lord for His unmerited favor!

As incredible as the gifts of healings may be, the workings of miracles is another amazing gift in its own right. We will cover that gift in the following chapter.

SUMMARY

The gifts of healings is:

1. A supernatural gift that brings or imparts healing to those who are sick.
2. Administered in various ways as directed by the Holy Spirit, but the default way is the laying on of hands.
3. A gift that heals any & every sickness.
4. Gradual.
5. Progressive.
6. Immediately imperceptible to the senses.
7. Distinctly different from the gift of workings of miracles.

Chapter 8

The Working(s) of Miracles

To another the working of miracles [by the same Spirit]...
(1 Corinthians 12:10, NKJV)

In this chapter, we will address the workings of miracles.

Looking at how the Apostle Paul presents the construct of the wording for the gift in its original language, we see that this gift is patterned after the discerning of spirits and the gifts of healings. Just as those gifts were in the plural, so is this gift in the plural form – workings of miracles. "Workings" and "miracles" reveal that the gift operates in various ways, and produces various types of miracles. Truly, God is a God of variety.

First, let us define the gift by looking at the words separately. "Workings" here in the Greek means "thing wrought, effect, and operation". "Miracles" in the Greek here is the word for dunamis (Strong's Concordance #1411). This is the common word for "miraculous power" in the New Testament. So the gift could be translated this way – "the gift of the things wrought by God's miraculous power".

As we saw in the previous gifts, this gift has a myriad of ways that the Spirit will lead a Spirit-filled believer to bring about the result He so seeks. I first want to class a few predominant types of miracles you can expect to occur with this gift (not an exhaustive list):

1. Immediate/Instant Healing
2. Expelling Demons
3. Creative Miracles
4. Raising of the Dead
5. Over Nature

The Miracle of Instantaneous Healing

The first one has to do with healing. In regards to the last gift, the gifts of healings, we saw that healing is gradual, progressive, and imperceptible. However, the workings of miracles is different when it comes to healing. This gift produces results instantly. There is no gradual effect. The working of miracles is a "now" gift. It is an in your face gift; A no holds bar kind of a gift. It is the type of gift where God says in a way, watch this – "Healing now!" Why? For faith is a now thing (Hebrews 11:1), and God lives within the ever present realm. His reality of time is the "eternal present", for this is determined from His name Jehovah (I AM) which denotes His essence being eternal.

God lives in the eternal present. Eternity is the realm of God. The earth realm on the other hand is confined to time: past, present, and future. When God deals with time, He deals with it out of His eternal reality, and that being eternal present. Hence, when we look at such a verse being Hebrews 13:8, which states, **"Jesus Christ is the same yesterday (past), today (present), and forever**

(future)." (NKJV) The verse states, **"Jesus Christ is"**, which speaks to His present existence in the eternal realm. He presently is alive and well seated upon His throne in Heaven. Notice what follows, **"the same yesterday, today, and forever."** This captures the earthen realm, which will be swallowed up by the eternal realm, for there will be new heavens and a new earth (Isaiah 65:17, 66:22, 2 Peter 3:13, Revelation 21).

Since He lives in the eternal present realm as God, Paul writes in Romans, **"God, who gives life to the dead and calls things into existence that do not exist."** (Romans 4:17, HCSB) God is not bound by time, because He controls it. Time is natural, and is bound to natural laws & functions, but God supersedes and superimposes His authority over time. Therefore, He can and does heal bodies instantly. Nothing is impossible to God!

Listen to John Sanford in *The Elijah Task*:

> "The law is relentless, for nothing changes it. Even God Himself does not break His own principles. If He did, His name would be Chaos rather than Father. What seems miracle and mystery to us is in truth operation of principles beyond the principles we know." (p. 111)

God can perform miracles, such as healing bodies instantly, for He is operating by principles beyond the principles we know naturally through the means of science.

In the previous chapter, we learned that the gifts of healings is imperceptible. However, the working of miracles is perceptible to the senses. When a person is the recipient of ministry by this gift, there is no wondering if there is a result. If the person was visibly sick, this gift will bring healing visibly. If the person could feel the pain, this gift will go into operation, and the person will sense the pain dissipate immediately.

The Miracle of Expelling Demons

Moving to the second class of miracles, the working of miracles manifests to expel demons. When this occurs, the gift of discerning of spirits will manifest to accompany it. This gift at times leads out in regards to the working of miracles to identify which spirit is at work and to be addressed by the expelling of the spirit from the individual's body. However, the gift of discerning of spirits does not always precede the working of miracles.

The operation of this gift was very evident in the life and ministry of Jesus, and that of the apostles of the first century. It is a reality even today.

Luke 4:31-35

> **In the synagogue there was a man with an unclean demonic spirit who cried out with a loud voice, "Leave us alone! What do You have to do with us, Jesus—Nazarene? Have You come to destroy us? I know who You are—the Holy One of God!" But Jesus rebuked him and said, "Be quiet and come out of him!" And throwing him down before them, the demon came out of him without hurting him at all.** (HCSB)

Acts 8:6-8

> **When the crowds heard Philip and saw the signs he performed, they all paid close attention to what he said. For with shrieks, impure spirits came out of**

many, and many who were paralyzed or lame were healed. So there was great joy in that city. (NIV)

Acts 16:16-18

"As we were on our way to the place of prayer, we were met by a slave girl who was possessed by a spirit of divination [claiming to foretell future events and to discover hidden knowledge], and she brought her owners much gain by her fortunetelling. She kept following Paul and [the rest of] us, shouting loudly, these men are the servants of the Most High God! They announce to you the way of salvation! And she did this for many days. Then Paul, being sorely annoyed and worn out, turned and said to the spirit within her, I charge you in the name of Jesus Christ to come out of her! And it came out that very moment." (AMP)

The Miracle of Creative Miracles

Also, in relation to healing, this gift not only heals instantly, but makes a person whole. I define in part that **wholeness is the body restored to where it is operating synergistically as it was meant to function**. But, this gift goes farther in its scope. It seeks to do that even when there is nothing there to restore. This gift truly expresses the character of God as Creator. Why?

Let us look at just a reference before getting into this point any further.

Matthew 15:31

So the multitude marveled when they saw the mute speaking, the maimed made whole, the lame walking,

and the blind seeing; and they glorified the God of Israel. (NKJV)

Notice what is said – "the maimed made whole". I looked at that and thought, "Wait a minute!" When you define the word maimed, it has two ways of seeing it:

1. A body part being disabled or injured
2. A body part being mutilated or missing

Leprosy was the disease that ruled and ravaged during the days of Jesus. It was a horrible disease, and greatly feared by the multitudes. It was like cancer today, but a communal disease. This disease of leprosy, once contracted, worked at eating the body till limbs started falling off the individual's body. Now, to heal the body meant that the disease was stopped. It was not permitted to progress any further, and it was removed. Therefore, this person would not die. They would live, but what sort of life is this person going to have with limbs missing? Paul says to desire the best gifts, and someone has been quoted as saying the best gift is the gift needed at the time. Where the gifts of healings healed the body, the working of miracles went beyond to restore the body parts missing or that have been ravaged by the disease.

> God is the One who created the earth-suit in the first place, and knows how to repair it.

Therefore, "whole" is synonymous with "God's creative power". The working of miracles is the power of God to create what may be presently absent from the picture. He in turn restores it to the person's body. How can He do that? He is the One who created the earth-suit in the first place, and knows how to repair it. He also knows how to restore what is missing from the storehouse of His immeasurable power (Habakkuk 3:4, Ephesians 1:19).

The Miracle of Raising the Dead

The next class is that of raising the dead. For many people, this is a stretch of the imagination. However, this is no stretch at all for God. Think about it. The Gospel hinges upon the fact of a supernatural occurrence – Jesus Christ died for the sins of the world, was buried, and was raised from the dead.

Paul said it this way:

I Corinthians 15:12, 20

> **Now if Christ is proclaimed as raised from the dead, how can some of you say, "There is no resurrection of the dead"...But now Christ has been raised from the dead, the first fruits of those who have fallen asleep.** (HCSB)

Verse twenty again states, "But now Christ has been raised from the dead." This miracle of raising the dead is not merely for a future occurrence, but is for the now present reality of our lives. We can experience the kingdom of God in respects to someone who has died, pray to God who gives life to the dead, and expect for them to revive. This was not strange to the Old Testament prophets, to Christ, to the apostles, nor to the first century saints.

Look at these ten following references regarding this form of miracle by the workings of miracles:

I Kings 17:17–24

> After this, the son of the woman who owned the house became ill. His illness became very severe until no breath remained in him. She said to Elijah, "Man of God, what do we have in common? Have you come to remind me of my guilt and to kill my son?" But Elijah said to her, "Give me your son." So he took him from her arms, brought him up to the upper room where he was staying, and laid him on his own bed. Then he cried out to the LORD and said, "My LORD God, have You also brought tragedy on the widow I am staying with by killing her son?" Then he stretched himself out over the boy three times. He cried out to the LORD and said, "My LORD God, please let this boy's life return to him!" So the LORD listened to Elijah's voice, and the boy's life returned to him, and he lived. (HCSB)

2 Kings 4:18–37

> Due to the length of the reference, please take this moment to read the passage before moving on in the chapter.

2 Kings 13:20, 21

> Then Elisha died and was buried. Groups of Moabite raiders used to invade the land each spring. Once when some Israelites were burying a man, they spied a band of these raiders. So they hastily threw the corpse into the tomb of Elisha and fled. But as soon as the body touched Elisha's bones, the dead man revived and jumped to his feet! (NLT)

Luke 7:12-17

> Just as He neared the gate of the town, a dead man was being carried out. He was his mother's only son, and she was a widow. A large crowd from the city was also with her. When the Lord saw her, He had compassion on her and said, "Don't cry." Then He came up and touched the open coffin, and the pallbearers stopped. And He said, "Young man, I tell you, get up!" The dead man sat up and began to speak, and Jesus gave him to his mother. Then fear came over everyone, and they glorified God, saying, "A great prophet has risen among us," and "God has visited His people." This report about Him went throughout Judea and all the vicinity. (HCSB)

Matthew 9:18, 19, 23-26

> As He was telling them these things, suddenly one of the leaders came and knelt down before Him, saying, "My daughter is near death, but come and lay Your hand on her, and she will live." So Jesus and His disciples got up and followed him.... When Jesus came to the leader's house, He saw the flute players and a crowd lamenting loudly. "Leave," He said, "because the girl isn't dead, but sleeping." And they started laughing at Him. But when the crowd had been put outside, He went in and took her by the hand, and the girl got up. And this news spread throughout that whole area. (HCSB)

John 11:38-44

> Then Jesus, angry in Himself again, came to the
> tomb. It was a cave, and a stone was lying against it.
> "Remove the stone," Jesus said.
>
> Martha, the dead man's sister, told Him, "Lord, he's
> already decaying. It's been four days." Jesus said to
> her, "Didn't I tell you that if you believed you would
> see the glory of God?" So they removed the stone.
> Then Jesus raised His eyes and said, "Father, I thank
> You that You heard Me. I know that You always hear
> Me, but because of the crowd standing here I said this,
> so they may believe You sent Me." After He said this,
> He shouted with a loud voice, "Lazarus, come out!"
> The dead man came out bound hand and foot with
> linen strips and with his face wrapped in a cloth. Jesus
> said to them, "Loose him and let him go." (HCSB)

Acts 9:36-42

> Now in Joppa there was a disciple named Tabitha
> (which translated in Greek is called Dorcas); this
> woman was abounding with deeds of kindness and
> charity which she continually did. And it happened
> at that time that she fell sick and died; and when they
> had washed her body, they laid it in an upper room.
> Since Lydda was near Joppa, the disciples, having
> heard that Peter was there, sent two men to him,
> imploring him, "Do not delay in coming to us." So
> Peter arose and went with them. When he arrived,
> they brought him into the upper room; and all the

widows stood beside him, weeping and showing all the tunics and garments that Dorcas used to make while she was with them. But Peter sent them all out and knelt down and prayed, and turning to the body, he said, "Tabitha, arise." And she opened her eyes, and when she saw Peter, she sat up. And he gave her his hand and raised her up; and calling the saints and widows, he presented her alive. It became known all over Joppa, and many believed in the Lord. (NASB)

Acts 20:7–12

On the first day of the week we came together to break bread. Paul spoke to the people and, because he intended to leave the next day, kept on talking until midnight. There were many lamps in the upstairs room where we were meeting. Seated in a window was a young man named Eutychus, who was sinking into a deep sleep as Paul talked on and on. When he was sound asleep, he fell to the ground from the third story and was picked up dead. Paul went down, threw himself on the young man and put his arms around him. "Don't be alarmed," he said. "He's alive!" Then he went upstairs again and broke bread and ate. After talking until daylight, he left. The people took the young man home alive and were greatly comforted. (NIV)

Romans 4:17

God, who gives life to the dead... (NKJV)

Hebrews 11:35a

Women received their dead raised to life again. (NKJV)

As you can see, this miracle of being raised from the dead is something the Bible testifies much about. It is no wonder why it would, because this is the great wonder that will take place at the return of Christ and at the last day where all will be raised from the dead (Daniel 12:2). Each one will be presented before God for judgment. It is not a hard thing for God to raise them now. Also, remember the words of Christ, "I am the resurrection and the life." Whenever and wherever the presence of Christ is in the midst, resurrection life and power is present.

Crowd Attractor

Moving on in describing the gift. The workings of miracles is a crowd attractor. My reason for saying this is because whenever this gift begins to manifest, crowds begin to form. This is a powerful gift in respects to its function. It creates a platform for the Gospel to be preached. If we were to further describe this gift, we would say it is likened to a net versus a fishing line. The fishing line will focus on catching one fish at a time. However, the working of miracles, is a gift that operates like a net. It is a gift that draws hundreds if not thousands of people at a time into the kingdom.

To see this aspect of the gift, let us look at a few biblical examples.

Luke 4:40-44

When the sun was setting, all those who had anyone sick with various diseases brought them to Him. As He laid His hands on each one of them, He would

heal them. Also, demons were coming out of many, shouting and saying, "You are the Son of God!" But He rebuked them and would not allow them to speak, because they knew He was the Messiah. When it was day, He went out and made His way to a deserted place. But the crowds were searching for Him. They came to Him and tried to keep Him from leaving them. But He said to them, "I must proclaim the good news about the kingdom of God to the other towns also, because I was sent for this purpose." And He was preaching in the synagogues of Galilee. (HCSB)

Jesus expelled a demon, and healed Simon Peter's mother of a fever. What transpired, multitudes of people flocked to where He was, even begging Him to stay when He desired to leave. What is interesting to note, however, is what the gift did – **it set the heart of the people to listen to the Gospel**. Whether they received the message or not, it created a willing audience.

Acts 2:1-7, 11, 12, 14-16, 36-39, 41

When the Day of Pentecost had fully come, they were all with one accord in one place. And suddenly there came a sound from heaven, as of a rushing mighty wind, and it filled the whole house where they were sitting. Then there appeared to them divided tongues, as of fire, and one sat upon each of them. And they were all filled with the Holy Spirit and began to speak with other tongues, as the Spirit gave them utterance. And there were dwelling in Jerusalem Jews, devout men, from every nation under heaven. And when this

sound occurred, the multitude came together, and were confused, because everyone heard them speak in his own language. Then they were all amazed and marveled, saying to one another, "Look, are not all these who speak Galileans...Cretans and Arabs—we hear them speaking in our own tongues the wonderful works of God." So they were all amazed and perplexed, saying to one another, "Whatever could this mean?"... But Peter, standing up with the eleven, raised his voice and said to them, "Men of Judea and all who dwell in Jerusalem, let this be known to you, and heed my words. For these are not drunk, as you suppose, since it is only the third hour of the day. But this is what was spoken by the prophet Joel..."Therefore let all the house of Israel know assuredly that God has made this Jesus, whom you crucified, both Lord and Christ." Now when they heard this, they were cut to the heart, and said to Peter and the rest of the apostles, "Men and brethren, what shall we do?" Then Peter said to them, "Repent, and let every one of you be baptized in the name of Jesus Christ for the remission of sins; and you shall receive the gift of the Holy Spirit. For the promise is to you and to your children, and to all who are afar off, as many as the Lord our God will call."...Then those who gladly received his word were baptized; and that day about three thousand souls were added to them. (NKJV)

From these references, we see that God pours out the Holy Spirit. This climactic event causes all those who were present to come and flock to where the saints were gathered. Peter recognizes that this miraculous event has created a platform for the Gospel to be preached, and so he begins to preach the Gospel. The outcome is that three thousand men, not including women and children, are saved.

Acts 3:7-12

> **Then Peter took the lame man by the right hand and helped him up. And as he did, the man's feet and ankles were instantly healed and strengthened. He jumped up, stood on his feet, and began to walk! Then, walking, leaping, and praising God, he went into the Temple with them. All the people saw him walking and heard him praising God. When they realized he was the lame beggar they had seen so often at the Beautiful Gate, they were absolutely astounded! They all rushed out in amazement to Solomon's Colonnade, where the man was holding tightly to Peter and John. Peter saw his opportunity and addressed the crowd. "People of Israel," he said, "what is so surprising about this? And why stare at us as though we had made this man walk by our own power or godliness?** (NLT)

This was a well-known man whom many knew in regards to his condition. It wasn't difficult to see that this man was infirmed in feet and legs. This very same man is who sat at the gate day in and day out begging for alms. This day, Peter and John stepped up to the plate, and declared him healed, and helped the man up. What happens next was that the man was miraculously healed.

The people who knew this lame man began to gather around to witness this sight of his healing by God's power. Peter watching the situation and recognized the gift created a platform again for the Gospel to be preached to an audience. The result was that two thousand men gave their lives to the Lord.

We can go on to list other events recorded in Acts that prove this point over and over again. The working of miracles is a dramatic gift for the sake of drawing large crowds of people, so that they may hear the glorious Gospel.

Territorial Breakthrough

One last thing I want to note regarding this gift. This gift is used by God to breakthrough various territories over run by demonic powers.

Mark 5:1-2, 9-10, 13, 19-20

> **Then they came to the other side of the sea, to the country of the Gadarenes. And when He had come out of the boat, immediately there met Him out of the tombs a man with an unclean spirit...They He asked him, "What is your name?" and he answered, saying, "My name is Legion; for we are many." Also he begged Him earnestly that He would not send them out of the country...And at once Jesus gave them permission. Then the unclean spirits went out and entered the swine (there were about two thousand); and the herd ran violently down the steep place into the sea, and drowned in the sea...However, Jesus did not permit him, but said to him, "Go home to your friends, and**

tell them what great things the Lord has done for you, and how He has had compassion on you." And he departed and began to proclaim in Decapolis all that Jesus had done for him; and all marveled. (NKJV)

As Spirit-filled believers operate within these gifts, they advance the kingdom of God. How is it understood that they advance the kingdom of God? Remember the words of Joel?

> **The Three Heavens:**
> **(2 Corinthians 12:2)**
>
> 1. **Natural Realm**
> 2. **Heavenly Realm**
> 3. **Realm of God**

Joel 2:30

And I will show wonders in the heavens and in the earth... (NKJV)

Acts 2:19

I will show wonders in heaven above and signs in the earth beneath... (NKJV)

These references do not merely refer to the first heaven (the natural realm above the earth – the stars, planets, and galaxies), but refer also to the heavens above the natural heaven.

The Three Heavens:

1. Natural Realm – Genesis 1:14-20, Joel 2:30-31
2. Heavenly Realm – 2 Corinthians 10:4-5, Ephesians 6:10-12
3. Realm of God (a.k.a. Paradise/Throne of God) – 2 Corinthians 12:2-4, Revelation 4:1-2

Apostles, prophets, and Spirit-filled believers are at times afforded such rights of entry into the heavenly realms to see what cannot be normally seen in the natural realm. The reason for this is so that they may operate from a vantage point, which enables them to attack the enemy in two realms to solidify their advance in the natural realm. You see, warfare is not just fought here on planet earth. It is fought in two realms: the heavenly realm & the natural realm.

A perfect and historical example is Moses and Joshua fighting the Amalekites. Moses went on the mountaintop, and he sent Joshua to fight in the valley. This was a physical picture of what actually was taking place in the spiritual realm. Moses denotes the battle being waged in the heavenly realm, while Joshua denotes the battle being waged in the natural realm. The one superseded the other, but both worked to secure victory that day. It is also important to note the importance of apostolic and intercessional ministry. There were only three on the mountain versus the hundreds or thousands fighting in the valley. As the three prayed, there was victory, but when the three stopped, defeat was imminent.

It is important to understand that these gifts are not for entertainment, but for a serious purpose. We are in a serious battle against forces in which we cannot see with the naked eye. Apostles, prophets, and Spirit-filled believers are granted such sight to see into the spiritual realm, so that they may function like Moses to secure the victory for those on the outpost of planet earth.

I want to state something here regarding these final days before the return of Christ and the consummation of all things. We are going to see apostles and prophets operating in a dimension as we have not seen before as they go about fulfilling their roles and assignments. There will be a greater display of this gift of the working of miracles in the coming days as more and more apostles and prophets walk in their full authority. The heavens will declare the glory of God, and the earth will testify in response to the goodness of God towards it. In the next chapter, we will cover the gift of prophecy.

SUMMARY

The gift of the working of miracles:

1. Is a gift that operates in different ways to manifest various types or classes of miracles.
2. Produces miracles that are instant, perceptible, dramatic, etc.
3. Produces various miracles: instant healings, casting out of demons, creative miracles, and raising of the dead.
4. Is a gift that produces territorial breakthroughs in regards to spiritual warfare in the heavens and on the earth.
5. Are a part of the arsenal of [some] apostles, prophets, and Spirit-filled believers.

Chapter 9

The Supernatural Gift of Prophecy

To another prophecy [by the same Spirit]... (1 Corinthians 12:10 NKJV)

We have now come to the third and last grouping within this study of the gifts of the Spirit.

We have looked at the two previous groups:

1. The Revelation Gifts
2. The Power Gifts

Now, we come to the Vocal Gifts. The list for the Vocal Gifts are:

1. Gift of Prophecy
2. Gift of Tongues
3. Gift of the Interpretation of Tongues

In this section, we are going to deal with the gift of prophecy. I will define the gift, so that we have a working knowledge of this most important gift. Then, I will give the purposes of the gift. Much can be said in regards to this gift, but what I have put forward here will be suffice to lay a foundation for the understanding of the gift of prophecy. I will address this gift somewhat different than how I have addressed the other gifts.

The gift of prophecy and the office of the prophet have been restored to the church. When I say restored, what I mean is that there is a resurgence of this gift in the Church. The gift has been in activity through the successive generations as noted in Church history to those whom the Lord would use by His choice/calling, their willingness, and their obedience. However, the gift operated in rarity like in the days of Eli.

1 Samuel 3:1

In those days the word of the LORD **was rare and prophetic visions were not widespread.** (HCSB)

This is how the gifts were during the time before the nineteen sixties. But now, we find that in the nineteen fifties, it was prophesied that God was going to restore the place of the prophetic. This prophecy is made mention of in *Prophet's and the Prophetic Movement* written by Dr. Bill Hamon (p. 48):

> "One of the rare occasions when a little encouragement was offered was in the early 1950's. A certain person who had an anointed ministry came and spoke to us of a coming day of glory and power and called it, 'the day of the prophets.' This person said that 'day' was thirty or more years down the road, for the Lord was preparing, even then, for greater things. The promise was that many mature prophetic ministries would spearhead a new day of restoration and revival."

This movement began in the nineteen eighties. The prophecy was true, and today, we have many prophets that have risen in the world for the purpose of God in preparing the Church for the second coming of Jesus Christ to planet earth (Malachi 4:5).

Let us now define what prophecy means. I am going to define the term by using biblical verses that give us its meaning, but I want to first define what it is not.

A. What is prophecy?

Prophecy is not...

1. Entertainment.

God deals with this aspect in regards to prophetic ministry in His words to His servant Ezekiel. He says:

Ezekiel 33:30-32

> **As for you, son of man, you've become quite the talk of the town. Your people meet on street corners and in front of their houses and say, "Let's go hear the latest news from God." They show up, as people tend to do, and sit in your company. They listen to you speak, but don't do a thing you say. They flatter you with compliments, but all they care about is making money and getting ahead. To them you're merely entertainment—a country singer of sad love songs, playing a guitar. They love to hear you talk (i.e., prophesy), but nothing comes of it. (MSG)**

When prophets speak, or when this gift is in operation, it is with divine purpose. God does not cause this gift to come about so that we can idly sit by, listen to a collection of nicely spoken words, and we leave their impressed by the verbal prowess of the speaker. No! Prophecy is very serious and important. When a prophet speaks, or this gift is in operation, God is seeking that something is to come about it – the people are to do what is spoken. Prophecy, therefore, evokes humble service and surrendered obedience unto the Lord.

When we do not understand the purpose of a thing, abuse is sure to occur. Also, when we do not understand the purpose of a thing, the blessing of God will be missed. Whenever prophecy goes forth, God is imparting various graces: the grace of faith, the grace of empowerment, the grace of knowledge, the grace of wisdom, and much more. Don't miss the grace!

2. Expository preaching.

I must make clear what I mean here. There is what we have in our services called "expository preaching". Then there is "prophetic preaching". Let's look at expository preaching using Scripture references that enforce this manner of the presentation of the Word.

Nehemiah 8:7-8

> **Jeshua, Bani, Sherebiah, Jamin, Akkub, Shabbethai, Hodiah, Maaseiah, Kelita, Azariah, Jozabad, Hanan, and Pelaiah, who were Levites, explained the Law to the people as they stood in their places. They read out of the book of the Law of God, translating and giving the meaning so that the people could understand what was read.** (HCSB)

2 Timothy 2:15

> **Study and be eager and do your utmost to present yourself to God approved (tested by trial), a workman who has no cause to be ashamed, correctly analyzing and accurately dividing [rightly handling and skillfully teaching] the Word of Truth.** (AMP)

2 Timothy 4:2

> **Herald and preach the Word! Keep your sense of urgency [stand by, be at hand and ready], whether the opportunity seems to be favorable or unfavorable. [Whether it is convenient or inconvenient, whether it is welcome or unwelcome, you as preacher of the Word are to show people in what way their lives are wrong.] And convince them, rebuking and correcting, warning and urging and encouraging them, being unflagging and inexhaustible in patience and teaching.** (AMP)

Expository preaching is giving the sense or meaning of a text. It is what Paul states, **"accurately dividing the Word of truth"**. Preaching is declaring or proclaiming the meaning of written Scripture. We need this sort of preaching more in this day where so much of what we have are messages which are likened to motivational speeches, and self-help information and guidance. Expository preaching is more than that, for it takes Scripture within its context (the culture, the time, the people, the language, the setting/environment in which the text was written, and gives the meaning that the text meant at the time, then bridges the gap of time by bringing the meaning to our modern context to pass along the principle and wisdom of God to the modern audience). This is a labor of love which (depending on the person) takes hours of study to effectually transmit this knowledge, and to present it orally to an assembly gathered for worship.

However, expository preaching is not prophecy. Though there is a prophetic element to expository preaching, it is not prophecy. Before giving what prophetic preaching is, let me first explain the prophetic element to expository preaching to make clear sense of what I mean. Years ago, in my homiletics course, my professor had one of my fellow classmates give his trial sermon. After the classmate concluded his message, our professor asked everyone what they received from his sermonic presentation. What was it that they heard? As he went down from one person to the next, each person had a distinctly different message, though we heard the very same sermon. None of what we stated was completely different, for there was a similarity to each one (a common thread), but there was a personal note each received from what was preached.

I'll say it again. From a sermon, each received a personal note from the message. This is the prophetic element in expository preaching. While you are delivering the meaning of the text, the Holy Spirit is taking a specific point from the message, and making it personal to the people who are gathered. That is why when I go to a church gathering, I go with two ears:

1. One to hear the speaker; hearing the preacher with my outer natural ear
2. One to hear the Holy Spirit; hearing the Spirit with my inner spiritual ear

Now, having that understanding, let us move to prophetic preaching. While expository preaching is the explanation of a text, prophetic preaching is the explanation of a prophecy. God gives a prophet a prophetic word, and then the prophet comes and delivers the prophecy through the medium/manner of a sermon. This is a greater dimension of preaching, because the person delivering the message is delivering a prophecy.

Let us look at this even further. The person is delivering a prophecy to the general assembly. This is not a personal prophecy, which means a prophet is ministering to a single person, but to a general assembly. It's a prophecy for everyone gathered. Thus, when the prophet is finished, everyone would have received a prophecy.

The next thing to note is that not only does the prophet multiply his ministry through giving a general prophecy through this medium, he explains the prophecy, so that all understand what God is actually saying. He is able to give all the flavor and colors of this prophecy, and all are able to grasp its practical meaning. All will leave the fog of vagueness, and walk into the glorious light of understanding and wisdom.

Lastly, prophetic preaching carries with it the same prophetic power that personal prophecy carries. When personal prophecy is uttered, there is a divine power that is released to bring about its fulfillment. There is a power that goes to work producing dynamic results that denote God is at work in conjunction to what was spoken (Jeremiah 1:12). As it states in Amos 3:7, **"Surely the Lord God will do nothing without revealing His secret to His servants the prophets."** (AMP). Therefore, when a prophet prophesies, it is a pronouncement of God about to do something. The same is true when a prophet preaches. He is making a general declaration. He is publicly proclaiming the will and work of God to His people in a profound manner that carries the supernatural grace of God to bring to pass His will in the earth through that local assembly.

So, prophetic preaching is expository preaching on steroids. What I mean by this expression is that prophetic preaching is a form of preaching that is **highly intensified** and **accelerates the grace of God** towards a particular goal that God has in mind in regards to His people. Prophecy is a medium for the power of God! How we need more of both expository preaching & prophetic preaching.

3. Witchcraft

When we look at the world, and even the words of the apostle Paul in first Corinthians, the world has its form of the supernatural. It is witchcraft. Even during the days of Moses, we find the Lord making reference of this reality to His people.

Deuteronomy 18:9-14

> **When you come into the land which the Lord your God is giving you, you shall not learn to follow the abominations of those nations. There shall not be found among you anyone who makes his son or his daughter pass through the fire, or one who practices witchcraft, or a soothsayer, or one who interprets omens, or a sorcerer, or one who conjures spells, or a medium, or a spiritist, or one who calls up the dead. For all who do these things are an abomination to the Lord, and because of these abominations the Lord your God drives them out from before you. You shall be blameless before the Lord your God. For these nations which you will dispossess listened to**

soothsayers and diviners; but as for you, the Lord your God has not appointed such for you. (NKJV)

I want to take a moment here to note the difference between one who practices witchcraft versus a prophet. The first distinction is found in the source by which they minister their craft. The witch does what he or she does by a demonic power (i.e., a familiar spirit) as noted in these references: Leviticus 20:27, 1 Samuel 28:7-8, 1 Chronicles 10:13, 33:6, Isaiah 19:3, 29:4, Jeremiah 2:8, 23:18, Acts 16:16. However, the prophet prophesies by the power of the Holy Spirit (2 Samuel 23:2, Acts 1:16, 6:10, 2 Peter 1:21).

The second distinctive mark is that those various forms of witchcraft is for hire, but the prophet is not. "For hire" means that the witch is paid money to use supernatural power to control or manipulate circumstances to reach a desired end. We have this example in the account of King Balak who hires Balaam to curse the children of Israel (Numbers 22-24; see Acts 8:9-13, 18-24). A prophet is not for hire, though he may be given an offering (1 Samuel 9:7-8). The way it operates is patterned after the way the priests earned a living (Leviticus 7:31–32).

One final thing that I will make mention here is that a witch will say and do what has been paid to be said and done. On the other hand, a prophet can only say or do what the Lord gives for him to share and accomplish – nothing more or less. Balaam, acting in this instance as God's prophet in Numbers 22, said it this way, **"If Balak were to give me his house full of silver and gold, I could not go against the command of the LORD my God to do anything small or great."** (Numbers 22:18, HCSB) He also says in verse thirty eight, **"Look, I have come to you, but can I say anything I want? I must speak only the message God puts**

in my mouth." (HCSB) These are the key differences between a witch and a prophet. There are more that we could pull upon, but it is suffice to state these few.

Now let us look at what prophecy is.

Prophecy is...

    1. Jesus giving testimony

Revelation 19:10

> **At this I fell at his feet to worship him. But he said to me, "Don't do that! I am a fellow servant with you and with your brothers and sisters who hold to the testimony of Jesus. Worship God! For it is the Spirit of prophecy who bears testimony to Jesus."** (NKJV)

Hebrews 1:1-2

> **In many separate revelations [each of which set forth a portion of the Truth] and in different ways God spoke of old to [our] forefathers in and by the prophets, [but] in the last of these days He has spoken to us in [the person of a] Son, Whom He appointed Heir and lawful Owner of all things, also by and through Whom He created the worlds and the reaches of space and the ages of time [He made, produced, built, operated, and arranged them in order].** (AMP)

Testimony is legal jargon to denote evidence being given as an official statement by a person who has actually seen or heard something. Prophecy is Jesus giving evidence of what He has seen and heard in the spiritual realm. What is so powerful is that the way He gives this evidence is by lifting the prophet or Spirit-filled believer into the spiritual realm to experience the same of what He sees and hears.

To help explain what I mean, the Lord has brought to my remembrance an example. Imagine you are a young child with your older brother at a parade. There are many people who have gathered to watch this parade. Unfortunately, you are unable to see and accurately hear the parade. You are missing the parade entirely. Then, you begin to tug on the pant-leg of your brother motioning to him to pick you up, so that you can see the parade and enjoy the experience of watching it. He obliges your request, picks you up, and places you upon his shoulders. You are now above the crowd, and are able to see with clarity the parade, and to hear devoid of all the interference of the many voices of those who towered above you.

This analogy helps us greatly to understand how we are able to receive the testimony of Jesus. The parade walking down the avenue are the things that are happening in the spiritual realm. The people standing along the sidewalks are the interference which makes seeing and hearing challenging. Your big brother is Jesus. Tugging on his pant-leg is prayer, which connects us to Him. He lifting us up is the operation of the Holy Spirit. This is what is spoken of in Scripture as "in the Spirit" (Ezekiel 37:1, Revelation 1:10).

Jesus placing you upon His shoulders is a powerful analogy to convey a powerful point. The Bible declares, **"For unto us a Child is born, unto us a Son is given; and the government**

> **In the spirit realm, a spirit-filled believer:**
>
> - **Sees things**
> - **Hears things**
> - **Receives things**

will be upon His shoulder..." (Isaiah 9:6 NKJV) The governance of God speaks of the dominant authority of the kingdom of God. The agent of the kingdom of God is the Holy Spirit (Luke 11). When our Big Brother picks us up, and places us upon His shoulders, what He in essence is doing is granting us the means to experience the supernatural authority and power of God in the manner of seeing and hearing the things that He sees and hears. We are connected to Him in such a way that we experience the reality of what the apostle Paul wrote to the Corinthians in the following verses.

2 Corinthians 12:3-4

> **And I know that this man—whether in the body or away from the body I do not know, God knows— was caught up into paradise, and he heard utterances beyond the power of man to put into words, which man is not permitted to utter.** (AMP)

Revelation 1:10, 12

> **I was in the Spirit on the Lords day, and I heard a loud voice behind me like a trumpet... I turned to see whose voice it was that spoke to me. When I turned I saw seven gold lampstands...** (HCSB)

Revelation 10:9-11

> **So I went to the angel and asked him to give me the little scroll. He said to me, "Take and eat it; it will be bitter in your stomach, but it will be as sweet as honey in your mouth." Then I took the little scroll from the angel's hand and ate it. It was as sweet as honey in my mouth, but when I ate it, my stomach became bitter.**

And I was told, "You must prophesy again about many peoples, nations, languages, and kings." (HCSB)

Three things to note here:

1. The spirit-filled believer **sees** things in the spirit realm
2. The spirit-filled believer **hears** things in the spirit realm
3. The spirit-filled believer **experiences and/or receives** things in the spirit realm

The testimony of Jesus is given whereby you see, hear, and receive into your heart. To receive into one's heart speaks of that which rises from within the spirit and into the mind. It speaks to that which moves you to action by what is within you by way of divine inspiration from that which is in the spirit realm. What is in the eternal realm moves you internally (inspiring various holy emotions), and motivates you to action in the earthen realm (Acts 7:23).

2. The proclamation of the will and activity of God.

Amos 3:7, 8

Indeed, the Lord GOD does nothing without revealing His counsel to His servants the prophets. A lion has roared; who will not fear? The Lord GOD has spoken; who will not prophesy? (HCSB)

I've mentioned this verse already, but I want to go a bit further in explaining this definition for prophecy. As we saw in definition 1, prophecy is God providing revelation for declaration. Verse eight of Amos three states, **"The Lord GOD has spoken; who will not**

prophesy?" Therefore, when you are afforded true revelation, God looks for its proclamation.

What God reveals is in the spiritual realm, He looks for its reality to manifest in the earthen realm through proclamation. The apostle Peter said, **"For we cannot but speak the things which we have seen and heard."** (Acts 4:20, NKJV) Revelation screams for proclamation. What is perceived requires a platform for proclamation. What is seen requires an avenue to be spoken.

When revelation is proclaimed, God is giving the means for that thing to come from the eternal realm to come into the natural realm. It is likened to the same reality in the creation account. God spoke, and it was established in the natural. We must capture what is said, **"Let there be..."** (Genesis 1:3) The word "let" is key. It speaks to the fact that there is something that is presently in opposition to what God wills to come forth. It further speaks to what currently takes up the space in which God now desires to be replaced by what He has spoken. Where there was darkness and emptiness, he now speaks with the desired intent of light and substance. Remember, Hebrews 11:3 states, **"By faith we understand that the worlds [during the successive ages] were framed (fashioned, put in order, and equipped for their intended purpose) by the word of God, so that what we see was not made out of things which are visible."** (AMP) The Message Version of Hebrews 11:3 puts it this way, **"By faith, we see the world called into existence by God's word, what we see created by what we don't see."**

Whenever prophecy goes forth, you are revealing the predetermined will of God. This means that God thought about this way before the foundation of the world. Also, you are revealing the activity of God. God gets personally involved in the reality of

His spoken word. It is His power that brings to pass and fulfills the prophetic word (2 Chronicles 6:4, 15). Whatever is prophesied reveals both realities (will & activity), and none can deny both. Numbers 29:19-20 states, **"God is not a man, that He should lie, nor a son of man, that He should repent. Has He said, and will He not do? Or has He spoken, and will He not make it good? Behold, I have received a command to bless; He has blessed, and I cannot reverse it."** (NKJV)

3. The display of the presence and power of the Spirit.

1 Corinthians 2:4

> **And my speech and my preaching were not with persuasive words of human wisdom, but in demonstration of the Spirit and of power...** (NKJV)

As with the other gifts of the Spirit, so it is with the gift of prophecy. The operation of the gifts manifests the Holy Spirit. This means that you are clearly and undeniably witnessing the Spirit of God. It is a disclosure of His presence, and also a display of His activity. Here it is through the gift of prophecy. This relates to His power. Divine power relates to the supernatural or the miraculous.

In regards to prophecy, 1 Corinthians 2:4 reveals a dimension of the miraculous. When we see a prophet or one operating in this gift of prophecy, we are witnessing the miraculous in verbal form. The words and vocabulary denote a world beyond our own. The way the words are put/framed together convey the mind of another personality beyond the person speaking. Yes, it is the words and vocabulary of the personality of the person, but the Holy Spirit chooses or selects sovereignly what words from the storehouse of that person He is speaking through. He is superimposing Himself through the person He is using in that moment, and it conveys a mind far superior to the person speaking.

Lastly, the words are embedded with a power that persuades the hearers. God's word moves people. There's a power that compels people, but this compelling force is not outward, but an inward one. 2 Corinthians 5:14 states, **"Christ's love controls us..."** (NLT) God's prophetic word urges us to move in the direction of what was prophetically spoken. This is not by force, but a gentle tug in a particular direction, which is the will of God.

4. The revelation of the mind and heart of God in regards to things past, present, and future; it is God's perspective concerning experiences.

1 Corinthians 2:16

For "who has known the mind of the LORD that he may instruct Him?" But we have the mind of Christ. (NKJV)

As we saw with Amos 3:7, here we see again the aspect of revelation. Prophecy is revelation from Jesus by the Holy Spirit to the glory of the God the Father. In Amos, we saw that the revelation had to do with the future doings of God. Here we see that it relates to the mind and heart of God. Another way of putting it is prophecy is the revelation of the thoughts and feelings of God. Amos deals with foretelling (the predictive element of God's revelation power), and Paul's words deal with forth-telling and includes foretelling as well.

In forth-telling, God is not necessarily dealing with the future, but He is addressing His perspective, His thoughts, and/or His intents, in regards to things that have happened in the past, or present (even those things that will happen in the future). Jeremiah 29:11 states,

"For I know the thoughts that I think toward you, says the Lord, thoughts of peace and not of evil, to give you a future and a hope." (NKJV) Psalm 139:17 states, "How precious to me are your thoughts, God! How vast is the sum of them!" (NIV)

It is not necessarily always the disclosure of what God will perform, but relates to how God views those things that occurred. He is giving a person through a prophetic mouthpiece His perspective that will give a different vantage in light of a particular occurrence.

Many times people experience things, and wonder, "Why did I have to go through that? What was that about?" Through the prophetic gift, He conveys His thought and feelings to the individual. At times, the person who is conveying the prophetic words will even be influenced by the Spirit to convey those emotions in his or her prophetic delivery. Is this always necessary? No, but sometimes, it helps the person to connect with God on that level, which will help in delivery.

5. Prophecy is God's command for creation.

Isaiah 48:6-8

> You have heard; See all this. And will you not declare it? I have made you hear new things from this time, even hidden things, and you did not know them. They are created now and not from the beginning; And before this day you have not heard them, lest you should say, "Of course I knew them." Surely you did not hear, surely you did not know; surely from long ago your ear was not opened. For I knew that you would deal very treacherously, and were called a transgressor from the womb. (NKJV)

Verse seven of Isaiah forty eight, in the Amplified, states it this way, **"They are created now [called into being by the prophetic word], and not long ago; and before today you have never heard of them, lest you should say, behold, I knew them!"** (AMP) Thus, prophecy brings into being things that do not presently exist. These things that are being created are:

- New Things
- Hidden Things
- Unknown Things
- Unheard Things

When God says, "I declare a new thing", He literally means a new thing. This is the thrilling reality of the prophetic. At times, God creates through the prophetic. God brings into being realities that have never existed in the earth. God is still in the creating business, for this is part of who He is – Creator God.

Ecclesiastes 1:9

> **What has been is what will be, and what has been done is what will be done; there is nothing new under the sun.** (HCSB)

Solomon is giving his human perspective of life under the sun. However, this cannot be said for God. Man is not creator, but God is!

Look at the next verse:

Jeremiah 31:22

> **For the LORD has created a new thing in the earth—a woman will encompass a man.** (NKJV)

What is God creating? Here in this text, He is creating not the cosmos (though scientists are showing things emerging in space all the time), but earthen realities or experiences. Realities that are opposite the nature of the preordered conditions as known to man in previous times. The natural order is a man encompassing a woman, but in this text God is creating something that is opposite the normal societal course of man on earth.

B. What are the Purposes or Benefits of Prophecy?

There are various key reasons for prophecy.

Edification

1 Corinthians 14:3

> **But he who prophesies speaks edification...to men.** (NKJV)

The Greek word for edification is oikodomeo (Strong's Concordance #3618), and it is defined as "to build up or improve (to turn something into profit) spiritually". It is prophetically bringing someone into a more desirable condition or state. Therefore, to edify means to make a person more useful, profitable, and advantageous in the Master's hand. God through the prophetic is seeking to build you up.

Exhortation

1 Corinthians 14:3

> **But he who prophesies speaks...exhortation...to men.** (NKJV)

The Greek word for exhortation is paraklēsis (Strong's Concordance #3874), and the word here is used to mean "to admonish or to encourage someone to action". God through the prophetic is seeking to stir you up to a particular action or activity.

Comfort

1 Corinthians 14:3

> **But he who prophesies speaks...comfort to men.** (NKJV)

The Greek word for comfort is paramythia (Strong's Concordance #3889), and the word here means "to console" a person. God through the prophetic is seeking to cheer you up; He is seeking to bring you to a more desirable and/or positive emotional state.

Prosperity

2 Chronicles 20:20

> **So they rose early in the morning and went out into the Wilderness of Tekoa; and as they went out, Jehoshaphat stood and said, "Hear me, O Judah and you inhabitants of Jerusalem: Believe in the LORD your God, and you shall be established; believe His prophets, and you shall prosper."** (NKJV)

The word **prosper** conveys that you are **empowered to conquer challenges** and **to overcome obstacles**. God equips you in such a way that one is able to conquer tasks or situations that tests [putting one under strain/stretch/stress] one's ability, and overcome things that blocks one's way or prevents or hinders one's progress.

What are the tools or equipment that the prophetic gives in order for one to prosper?

a. Vision – a specific God-ordained goal
b. Strategy – a knowledgeable plan to achieve a specific God-ordained goal
c. Tactic – the practical steps taken designed to achieve that specific God-ordained goal

Revelation

Isaiah 42:9

> **Behold, the former things have come to pass, and new things I now declare; before they spring forth I tell you of them.** (AMP)

Isaiah 44:7

> **Who is like Me? Let him [stand and] proclaim it, declare it, and set [his proofs] in order before Me, since I made and established the people of antiquity. [Who has announced from of old] the things that are coming? Then let them declare yet future things.** (AMP)

Isaiah 46:10

> **Declaring the end and the result from the beginning, and from ancient times the things that are not yet done, saying, My counsel shall stand, and I will do all My pleasure and purpose...** (AMP)

God grants revelation regarding future matters, so that the Church may be informed of what is to take place (Acts 11:27-30).

In regards to personal prophecy, God affords a person knowledge of His will and activity, so the person can have the edge in regards to those matters (Acts 21:10-14).

Creation

Isaiah 48:6-8

> **You have heard [these things foretold], now you see this fulfillment. And will you not bear witness to it? I show you specified new things from this time forth, even hidden things [kept in reserve] which you have not known. They are created now [called into being by the prophetic word], and not long ago; and before today you have never heard of them, lest you should say, Behold, I knew them! Yes, you have never heard, yes, you have never known; yes, from of old your ear has not been opened. For I, the Lord, knew that you, O house of Israel, dealt very treacherously; you were called a transgressor and a rebel [in revolt] from your birth.** (AMP)

When prophecy goes forth, it is like when God spoke in the beginning, saying, **"Let there be light."** The result was light. This is the powerful reality of the prophetic — it creates things. God creates ex nihilo (i.e., out of nothing), and so many times God will move upon a prophet to prophesy things into being or reality that did not exist before. Prophecy is God's command for creation, or in other words, manifestation of what does not exist presently in the natural.

The gift of prophecy is a much needed gift, but misunderstood by many. This gift of prophecy is a gift which the Lord ranks very high in the arsenal of the Church through the agency of His Spirit. But, so many in the Church refuse to allow this gift its expression, and when it does express itself, it is held in contempt. The apostle Paul says, **"Do not treat prophecies with contempt."** (NIV) My prayer and hope is that this book will be a means of helping the gifts come from a place of contempt to a place of honor and reverence within the Church. Prayerfully, that is exactly what has been taking place as you have been reading through these pages upon the previous gifts.

I would like to end this chapter with two pastoral testimonies regarding prophecies the Lord led me to give which helped these pastors in their personal matters of life and ministry.

Pastor Dwayne Wright's Testimony

Elder Pierre gave my wife and I a prophetic word about our ministry and son.

I've been pastoring over the last five years. It has been a tough, but rewarding road to serve God's people. God knows how to send a word of encouragement and confirmation in the right time to strengthen us on this journey of faith.

Over a couple of years, my wife and I had been praying privately about moving the ministry to a different location, and we didn't share this information with anyone. Elder Pierre gave us a word of knowledge and wisdom that revealed our prayers and God's will concerning us moving the ministry; also the decisions that were before us. The Lord gave him insight into what we had been crying out to the Lord. God used Elder Pierre to minister to us at a time when we were facing some tough decisions.

He continued by saying the Lord was preparing us to be parents. At the time, we wanted to wait at least another year before we began our family. We didn't know it, but when he gave us that word about us becoming parents, my wife was pregnant.

Pastor Donna Mosley's Testimony

In August of 2014, Elder Evans preached at my church. It was the first time that he had ever visited our church, and prior to his coming, we had not communicated in 5 years since. I relocated to PA and had begun pastoring there. It has been on my heart for the entire 5 years to invite him, because I had experienced his ministry while living in New Jersey.

When he came, he prophesied to me that I was getting ready to go on a long awaited vacation. He had no knowledge that, number one, I had not been on a vacation since planting Balm Church in December 2008, and two, that the week before I had requested money from our board of directors to take a long needed vacation. The board had just given me two thousand dollars to take a vacation, the week before Elder Evans came, but the vacation had not been planned yet. Elder Evans saw palm trees and sand. Well as I searched for a place to go, I had no desire to travel to any island. Also, I felt that I could not afford an island vacation at the time.

I was having such difficulty trying to decide where to go, that I came close to settling for the Jersey shore. My son, who is an elder at our church, remembered that I had always wanted to visit the Holy Land Experience in Florida and suggested it to me. I was elated. I don't know why I had not been able to think of that myself, but the idea of the Holy Land had never come to mind during the time of planning. The Lord worked out a beautiful trip for us which was more than a vacation, but a time of restoration. Elder Evans saw our trip in the spirit, and we were comforted in knowing that our vacation was God's will; and therefore, our vacation was an unforgettable experience for my husband and I.

Let us move to the final two gifts of the grouping and of the list of the gifts: the gift of tongues and the gifts of the interpretation of tongues.

In the next chapter, we are going to look at the gift of tongues.

SUMMARY

The gift of prophecy:

1. Is not entertainment, expository preaching, nor witchcraft.
2. Is Jesus giving testimony, proclamation of God's will and work.
3. Is the display of the Spirit's presence and power.
4. Is the revelation of God's mind and heart.
5. Is God's command for creation.
6. Has benefits, and they are: edification, exhortation, comfort, prosperity, revelation, and creation of things in the natural realm.

Chapter 10

The Different Kinds of Tongues

To another different kinds of tongues [by the same Spirit]...
(1 Corinthians 12:10 NKJV)

When we think of tongues in Pentecostal and Charismatic circles, we think of them as the evidence of being filled with the Spirit, and beyond that, simply a devotional thing we do when we "feel the Spirit". We must begin to view tongues with a clearer perspective and understanding, because tongues is more than the evidence of the baptism, and more than just a reactionary response to a feeling. Matter of fact, tongues is "an" evidence and not "the" evidence of being filled with the Spirit. This is the first misunderstanding I want to address before I move into the body of this chapter.

A Misunderstanding

When we look at the birth and inauguration of the Church of Jesus Christ, we see that the believers, numbering 120, were waiting for the promise of the Spirit. The Lord Jesus told them to wait in the city of Jerusalem, for the Spirit would descend upon them in power. In obedience, they waited. Isaiah 40:31 states, **"But those who wait for the Lord [who expect, look for, and hope in Him] shall change and renew their strength and power..."** (AMP) The "wait" in the Hebrew tongue is qavah (Strong's Concordance #6960), and it properly means "to twist or to bind a rope". When you bind two or three cords to make a rope, you in essence double or triple the strength of the individual cords. Ecclesiastes 4:12, in part, states, **"A cord of three strands is not quickly (i.e., easily) broken."** (NIV) The rope is strong due to the many-corded reality that has made the cords a rope. It has reinforced strength.

This same Hebrew word means "to expect". When reading the verse, it would say, "Those who expect the Lord..." The word expect means to hope, and so looking further we understand to wait means "to fix one's hope on the Lord and His aid." (Thayer's Lexicon) We have three components in regards to this one Hebrew word:

1. Twist (cords in making a strong rope)
2. Expectation (of the Lord's presence)
3. Hope (in the Lord's aid/provision)

Put these three together, what you have is "waiting upon the Lord means that you have fixed your hope in Him in such a way, that you grow stronger in your expectation of His presence & aid as time progresses, and that nothing will nor can move you from your fixed position."

These believers were there waiting. Day one, then day two, and then day six passed. They remained there together knowing that God was faithful to keep His word. They had banded together to wait upon the Lord, and they were not going anywhere. He had promised

His aid in this mission He surrendered over to them. They were going to wait for this provision of His grace.

What were they doing during these days to past the time? The Bible verses following will help us to know the answer to this question.

Luke 24:52, 53

> **And they worshiped Him, and returned to Jerusalem with great joy, and were continually in the temple praising and blessing God. Amen.** (NKJV)

Acts 1:13, 14

> **And when they had entered, they went up into the upper room where they were staying: Peter, James, John, and Andrew; Philip and Thomas; Bartholomew and Matthew; James the son of Alphaeus and Simon the Zealot; and Judas the son of James. These all continued with one accord in prayer and supplication, with the women and Mary the mother of Jesus, and with His brothers.** (NKJV)

Acts 1:16, 17

> **Men and brethren, this Scripture had to be fulfilled, which the Holy Spirit spoke before by the mouth of David concerning Judas, who became a guide to those who arrested Jesus; for he was numbered with us and obtained a part in this ministry.** (NKJV)

The threefold-cord that strengthened them in their waiting till the aid of the Lord appeared was prayer, worship, and meditation. If we are going to wait upon the Lord, we must understand the place of these three things that help us in the process.

This further teaches that waiting upon God is not a passive idle sitting on the sidelines. However, waiting upon the Lord

Threefold Cord of Waiting:

- **Prayer**
- **Worship**
- **Meditation**

is actually an active reality whereby while waiting for something to manifest that He has promised. We are actively enthralled in worship, engaged in prayer, and diligently studying God's word. All of this primes (i.e., makes a thing ready) our whole human frame or personality to receive whatever it is that God will bring into our lives. We will be in such a state of readiness, and we will not miss His blessed visitation and the reception of His provision.

On the Day of Pentecost, the Holy Spirit came in with great power upon those gathered, and they were **all** filled with Him. It was an amazing thing. There was the hurricane type winds, the shaking and quaking of the building, the winds filling the room where they were, the appearance of fire, then the fire separating into tongues of fire, and then resting/settling upon each of the 120 gathered. Then each in whom the fire rested were then filled with the Spirit, and finally each believer began to speak in other tongues. These were known languages of the people who had come from all over to keep the Feast of Weeks or Pentecost.

This speaking forth these strange known languages (unknown to them) were not a silent type of speech, but it was loud and clear what they gave expression to. They were not shy or embarrassed in light of what they received, but bold, confident it its origins, and overjoyed at its reception. They were so loud that the people from the streets heard them speaking their languages. This became a draw factor, and Peter seeing this occurring began to preach the Gospel of

Jesus Christ. The result? Three thousand men (not including women and children) were won to Christ that day! What a birth! What an inauguration! Only God could have done it that way.

From this historical account, we have built a doctrine. The doctrine is that tongues is "the" evidence of being filled with the Spirit. To properly discern aright regarding the evidence of being filled, we must look at each passage in the book of Acts to get a clear look at this doctrine.

Filled with the Spirit

Acts 2:1-4

> **When the Day of Pentecost had fully come, they were all with one accord in one place. And suddenly there came a sound from heaven, as of a rushing mighty wind, and it filled the whole house where they were sitting. Then there appeared to them divided tongues, as of fire, and one sat upon each of them. And they were all filled with the Holy Spirit and began to speak with other tongues, as the Spirit gave them utterance. (NKJV)**

Acts 4:31

> **And when they had prayed, the place where they were assembled together was shaken; and they were all filled with the Holy Spirit, and they spoke the word of God (i.e., the Gospel) with boldness. (NKJV)**

Acts 9:17, 18

> **And Ananias went his way and entered the house; and laying his hands on him he said, "Brother Saul, the**

Lord Jesus, who appeared to you on the road as you came, has sent me that you may receive your sight and be filled with the Holy Spirit." Immediately there fell from his eyes something like scales (i.e., healing), and he received his sight at once; and he arose and was baptized. (NKJV)

Acts 10:44–46

While Peter was still speaking these words, the Holy Spirit fell upon all those who heard the word. And those of the circumcision who believed were astonished, as many as came with Peter, because the gift of the Holy Spirit had been poured out on the Gentiles also. For they heard them speak with tongues and magnify (i.e., worshipped) God. Then Peter answered... (NKJV)

Acts 13:48, 49, 52

Now when the Gentiles heard this, they were glad and glorified the word of the Lord. And as many as had been appointed to eternal life believed. And the word of the Lord was being spread throughout all the region. And the disciples were filled with joy and with the Holy Spirit. (NKJV)

Acts 19:5, 6

When they heard this, they were baptized in the name of the Lord Jesus. And when Paul had laid hands on them, the Holy Spirit came upon them, and they spoke with tongues and prophesied. (NKJV)

Having looked at these few references in the book of Acts we can say that tongues is the **predominant** manifestation of one being filled with the Spirit, but it is **not the only** evidence (i.e., obvious to the eye) of being filled. The others that are shown from these references are:

1. Preaching the word of God with boldness
2. Healing
3. Worship
4. Joy
5. Prophecy

So, we mustn't put God in a box (of confinement and limitation) to say that a person is not filled because there was no "speaking with other tongues".

I have prayed for my God-sister to be filled with the Spirit some years ago. That night she did not "speak with other tongues". I went home, and we met together again not too many days afterward, and I heard her speaking with tongues as we bowed our heads to pray. I wondered when did this happen, but now I realize that there are other ways of discerning if a person is filled initially.

Tongues, however, will be a forthcoming reality if not present initially. This was confirmed as I watched a well-known seasoned prophet minister to a gentleman the baptism with the Holy Spirit. He said by the count of three, the gentleman would be filled with the Spirit. He said it was going to be powerful, and I waited with exuberant expectation to see what tremendous reception this was going to be. And as I watched, he counted three, and then to my amazement and disappointment, nothing. I could see the prophet was moved, but the gentleman he prayed for was not moved. His hands were up, but that was the most I saw of him do anything in the process. The prophet further stated that he had just received the Holy Spirit, and get this, that he would speak in tongues not to many days from now. I sat there and was floored. I thought, "He missed God here. He does not know how to minister the baptism with the Holy Spirit." My doctrinal stance was shaken and disturbed, and rightfully so! It needed to be shaken, because I had come to a place where I had boxed God in. God does not work within our nice doctrinal frames and denominational parameters that we make. He is God! He is a Person having myriad of ways of doing things, which He does well.

From that day it was confirmed within my own heart that tongues is not "the" evidence of being filled, but "a" predominant manifestation of being filled with Him. You see, the Lord had already been dealing with me on this fact. I had even mentioned this a time or two in teaching the word, but whenever it came time to minister the gift, I would look for the evidence – tongues. I have a better understanding now by the Scriptures. Even more, by the Holy Spirit, one can discern where a person is in the process of being filled. It's amazing!

My wife and I were ministering to a friend to receive the baptism with the Spirit. As we tarried (i.e., worshipping [the bowing down of the flesh in humble surrender to commune with God by the human spirit] through the process of receiving) with her, I could see or discern actually where she was. The imagery I was granted to help me was her coming to the side of a river bank, and she put her toe into the water to test it. When I saw that, I knew that she was there at the point, but was a bit timid or frightful. We coached her through, and she would get into the Spirit, and come back out due to her mind, which would get in the way. This went on a few times until she began to speak with other tongues. I know that she received, but speaking with other tongues is going to be a work in progress for her. The reason being is due to what Paul writes in 1 Corinthians 14:14.

Paul says it this way:

> **For if I pray in a tongue, my spirit prays, but my understanding is unfruitful.** (NKJV)

> **For if I pray in an [unknown] tongue, my spirit [by the Holy Spirit within me] prays, but my mind is unproductive [it bears no fruit and helps nobody].** (AMP)

Principally, the mind trips us up. It short circuits our ability to receive and operate in the Spirit.

Let us now move to define the gift.

When you look at the construct of the gift in its original language, something interesting emerges that I would like to take the time to treat, so that you can see the diverse ability of the Spirit. There are two Greek words that make up the identification of the gift: genos (i.e., kinds) and glossa (i.e., tongues). The understanding of genos is related to our English word for genes, species, or class (Matt. 13:47, 17:21, Mk 9:29, 1 Cor. 12:10, 28, 14:10). Therefore, there are different classes of tongues by which the Spirit can speak through us. Furthermore, glossa is defined as "the gift of men who, rapt in an ecstasy and no longer quite masters of their own reason and consciousness, pour forth their glowing spiritual emotions in strange utterances, rugged, dark, disconnected, and quite unfitted to instruct or to influence the minds of others."[2]

There are different sorts of tongues in the cosmos. Tongues can either be known or unknown languages. In 1 Corinthians 13:1, Paul speaks of the languages of men. There are languages of men that are so ancient and have not been in use for centuries. Then there are languages that are present today that most people have never heard. Are you aware that there are African groups that use clicks as their known language, and it is a viable learned language? Paul also speaks of the languages of angels (i.e., holy angels, and unholy spirits).

However, tongues, is a supernatural language that cannot be taught or learned to be spoken. I am always appalled when I hear from others how they were at a service, and the altar workers were leading people into the baptism with the Spirit. They over heard the altar worker saying "say this" or "say it like this". You may speak in tongues while leading someone else, but you do not direct them to form the words and sounds you are speaking. The tongues you are speaking come from your own spirit. It is borne out of the intimate connection you have with the Spirit. You cannot fabricate intimacy!

It is the same thing as what was stated by God in regards to the anointing oil:

Exodus 30:30-33

> **Then anoint Aaron and his sons. Consecrate them as priests to me. Tell the Israelites, "This will be my holy anointing oil throughout your generations." Don't pour it on ordinary men. Don't copy this mixture**

---

[2] http://www.blueletterbible.org/lang/lexicon/lexicon.cfm?Strongs=G1100 &t=NKJV

to use for yourselves. It's holy; keep it holy. Whoever mixes up anything like it, or puts it on an ordinary person, will be expelled. (MSG)

To copy the mixture of the anointing oil brought grave consequences. And so, we must not treat the gift of tongues with frivolity nor as something ordinary. Leading someone into the experience of the baptism where tongues comes about is a most intimate reality. The baptism with the Holy Spirit is second to being born again. Therefore, we must treat it (i.e., the experience) as God would have it treated – sacred intimacy between Himself and His bride.

Tongues is the language of the spirit man in communion with God by the help or assistance of the Holy Spirit. This is why tongues cannot be fabricated. It is not a man thing, but a God thing in man.

Acts 2:4

And they were all filled with the Holy Spirit and began to speak with other tongues, as the Spirit gave them utterance. (NKJV)

Acts 2:1-4

Then, like a wildfire, the Holy Spirit spread through their ranks, and they started speaking in a number of different languages as the Spirit prompted them. (MSG)

Tongues is the work of the Spirit in and through you. Tongues, in an unknown language, is communication that is directed to God, and is understood by God alone. Paul says, **"For he who speaks in a tongue does not speak to men but to God, for no one**

understands him; however, in the spirit he speaks mysteries."
(I Corinthians 14:2 NKJV)

I want to share here a way to understand tongues that God has given me, and I pray it helps you to understand tongues a bit better and appreciate its blessing.

A Secured Line

Praying in tongues is likened to speaking with someone on a secured line. What is a secured line you may ask? A secured line is a telephone that is encrypted to protect the speakers and their conversation from eavesdropping and manipulation by someone secretly in the middle of that conversation. God, in His infinite wisdom, in understanding the times in which we live in (Ephesians 2:2), has given us a tool for spiritual warfare. Matter of fact, if you look at the notable passage on spiritual warfare, you will find Paul calling for believers to pray in the Spirit (i.e., tongues).

Ephesians 6:17, 18

> **And take the helmet of salvation, and the sword of the Spirit, which is the word of God; praying always with all prayer and supplication in the Spirit (i.e. tongues), being watchful to this end with all perseverance and supplication for all the saints...** (NKJV)

We have an adversary, the man-in-the-middle — Satan, who seeks to intercept our prayers (Daniel 10:12-14). However, in this dispensation, we have been given something which he cannot intercept. It is a powerful tool that many believers still do not grasp concerning its full potential. Tongues is no little thing within the kingdom of God. God has been trying to prepare us for this phenomenon for centuries before Pentecost in Acts (e.g., Isaiah 28:11-12). Before Christ's passion and ascension, He stated tongues would be a part of the arsenal attached to His name in spiritual warfare – **"And these signs will accompany those who believe: In My name they will drive out demons; they will speak in new languages..."** (Mark 16:17, NKJV) Notice the connection between the expelling of demons with speaking with tongues. Tongues has a serious role in spiritual warfare.

Satan and demons cannot stand tongues, because it is something that they cannot hack. Authentic tongues is un-hackable! Praying in tongues is encrypted communication with God. If prayer is likened to talking on a telephone with God, then tongues is God's secured hotline. This is the emergency phone that is connected directly to His throne. Tongues is on a frequency so beyond all other frequencies, Satan can only simply wait and see what transpires as a result. With tongues, he cannot raise up a preemptive strike. He simply has to wait, but by that time, it is already too late. Damage has occurred to his plan and kingdom. God has done what we have communicated to Him in tongues.

Again, tongues is a connection that is encrypted, and the only way to gain access is to break the code. The only Person who has the code is the Holy Spirit. He only reveals it to those who are disciples (Isaiah 50:4). This is getting into the aspect of interpretation, which is the next chapter. We will leave that for then, but we need to understand that tongues is a powerful reality afforded to

Disciple of the Spirit

A disciple of the Spirit is one whose ear has been awakened or activated by the Spirit to hear what He is saying, so that this disciple may have the tongue of the learned and trained – one who can speak a prophetic word in season to him who is weary.

the Church. We must capitalize on its use to advance the kingdom of God. Tongues is not given so that we can have some euphoric feeling, but to draw wisdom on what to do in advancing God's kingdom.

Let me now end this chapter with giving the different classes of tongues.

Different Classes of Tongues

(This is not an exhaustive list.)

1. Tongues of Thanksgiving – 1 Corinthians 14:16-17

    These tongues are when one prays/speaks in the unknown language communicating thanksgiving to God for what He has done. Furthermore, as David states in Psalm 100:4, **"Enter into His gates with thanksgiving..."** (NKJV), we enter into the presence of God through tongues of thanksgiving.

2. Tongues of Praise – 1 Chron. 25:3, 7, Acts 2:11, 1 Cor. 14:15, Eph. 5:18-19, Col. 3:16

    These tongues are when one prays in an unknown language communicating praise to God for who He is. David says in Psalm 100:4, **"Enter into His gates with thanksgiving, and into His courts with praise."** (NKJV) Tongues of praise are not just for a time of verbal acknowledgment of God's identity and honor, but a means of ushering you into the supernatural courts or tribunals of God (Psalm 84:, 10, 92:13, 135:2; c.f. Jeremiah 23:18, 22). In these courts, one receives revelation of God's counsel in regards to various matters on planet earth.

3. Tongues of Intercession – Romans 8:26-28

These tongues are for the sake of praying for others. Intercession can be done in one's known language, but when it is done in an unknown tongue, intercession then goes to higher levels of intercession. The spirit of man is thus lifted beyond the limitations of one's mind and knowledge regarding the realities of what one is praying about. Paul's words in Romans are true in regards to this point, for he says in Romans 8:26, **"Likewise the Spirit also helps in our weaknesses. For we do not know what we should pray for as we ought, but the Spirit Himself makes intercession for us with groanings which cannot be uttered."** (NKJV) The Spirit of God helps us in the ministry of intercession by granting us the very words in tongues to pray to God our Father in the name of Jesus. We bypass earthly carnal limitations, and move into a realm and dimension in the spirit whereby our impact is more impactful and dynamic in its working.

4. Tongues of Edification – 1 Corinthians 14:2, Jude 20

These are tongues for the purpose of building you up to a place conducive to spiritual ministry. Another way of describing this is what Paul said to Timothy in 1 Timothy 1:6, **"Therefore, I remind you to stir up the gift of God which is in you..."** (NKJV) I do this often prior to ministering in the gifts, because it primes my whole nature; it gets me ready to co-labor with the Spirit of God.

5. Tongues of Prophecy – 1 Corinthians 14:5 (corporate setting), 13 (individual)

These are tongues which precede the word of prophecy. As one prays in tongues, he or she is priming or edifying themselves to receive a word from the Lord. Thus, praying in tongues affords one the ability of hearing and receiving spiritual information from God through the Holy Spirit, which one can communicate to another or others.

6. Tongues of Rest and Refreshing – Isaiah 28:12, cf.1 Corinthians 14:21

This is where as you pray in tongues that the Holy Spirit refreshes by bringing you into a place of restfulness within your soul. The more you pray in tongues, the more refreshment comes to you as the presence of God settles you. It is a beautiful time in the holiness of God (1 Chronicles 16:29, 2 Chronicles 20:21, Psalm 29:2).

7. Tongues of Revelation – 1 Corinthians 14:30

These are tongues that afford a Spirit-filled believer revelation or the disclosure of the will, way, and work of God. As one prays in tongues, the Spirit will bring to his or her understanding what was hidden from them and others. This disclosure will be about the 3 levels of God's will: His good will, His acceptable will, and/or His perfect will (Romans 12:2). Also, the Spirit will bring illumination to one regarding God's way (i.e., His method, mode, system, technique, or tactic). Lastly, as one prays in tongues, the Spirit will afford him or her the opportunity to see how God will work to bring about His will. He will give that one insight into His power and involvement in bringing about what His determined will in the earth.

8. Tongues of Warfare – Ephesians 6:18

These are tongues in which the Spirit directs our spirit to pray against demonic beings and forces in the supernatural realm. This is a form of contending with demons and demonic principalities who endeavor to carry out Satan's will. When we pray in tongues, we are countering those desires of Satan, and supernaturally enforcing the will of God. Tongues of warfare can occur while even praying for someone who asks for prayer, and all of the sudden, your prayer language changes to a sort where you are angry. (This is the emotion of God expressing itself through you as you pray in the Spirit.) Usually, this happens in conjunction to the operation of the gift of discerning of spirits. I have experienced it at times in said manner where I would be shown a demon spirit, and the sense of God's emotion or feeling would rise, and my prayer language would match the emotion.

9. Tongues of Angels – 1 Corinthians 13:2

This is when you are speaking in tongues, and it is directed to an angel of either class. There are two classes of angels: holy angels and unholy angels. The Holy Spirit will at times (a rarity) empower you to speak in the language of a demon to address that spirit. Paul states a powerful truth that we need to see. In 1 Corinthians 2:7-8, he states, **"But we speak the wisdom of God in a mystery, the hidden wisdom which God ordained before the ages for our** glory, which none of the rulers of this age knew; for had they known, they would not have crucified the Lord of glory." Who are these rulers of this age? Is Paul referencing the Roman soldiers that crucified Jesus? Or, is Paul speaking of the Jewish rulers who handed Jesus over to the Roman governor Pontius Pilate? Let's see this term or phrase which he uses here to understand who Paul is referencing. He states in Ephesians 3:10, "God's purpose in all this was to use the church to display his wisdom in its rich variety to all the unseen rulers and authorities in the heavenly places." (NLT) Paul further states in Ephesians 6:12, "For we do not wrestle against flesh and blood, but against principalities, against powers, against the rulers of the darkness of this age, against spiritual hosts of wickedness in the heavenly places." (NKJV) It is obvious here that Paul in 1 Corinthians 2:7-8 is not referencing human agents, but demonic forces that were working behind the scenes. They were the real culprits who crucified the Lord of glory. We speak in tongues or we speak mysteriously by way of tongues to the rulers of this present Dark Age.

10. Tongues of Men – 1 Corinthians 13:2

This is when the Holy Spirit will at times move upon you to speak to men (the various languages of men on earth: past or present) to communicate a message from God to them. We see this happen on the day of Pentecost (Acts 2:7-12). The purpose of this is to serve as a sign and wonder to men who are unbelievers that they may know that God has spoken to them (Isaiah 28:11; c.f. 1 Corinthians 14:22). Furthermore, this creates a platform for a practical presentation of the Gospel, for the consciousness of men have been awakened by this supernatural phenomena.

This list captures the major kinds or classes one may find when praying or speaking in tongues. Each has their distinct powerful purpose. We must begin to truly immerse ourselves in praying and speaking in tongues. There will be much more done for the kingdom of heaven if we do so. So, as Paul stated about himself regarding tongues, **"I thank God, I speak in tongues more than you all..."** (1 Corinthians 14:18, NASB) I say we follow his example, and pray in tongues more.

In the next chapter, we will address the next gift – the gift of the interpretation of tongues.

SUMMARY

The gift of tongues:

1. Is the predominant manifestation of one being filled with the Spirit, but it is not the only evidence (i.e., obvious to the eye) of being filled.
2. Can be either known languages or unknown languages.
3. Is the language of the spirit man in communion with God by the help or assistance of the Holy Spirit.
4. Is likened to speaking with God on a secured line.
5. Is a connection that is encrypted, and the only way to gain access is to break the code. The Holy Spirit is the code-breaker.

6. Is a gift which Satan and demons cannot bear, because it is something that they cannot hack.

7. Has different classes: thanksgiving, praise, intercession, warfare, edification, prophecy, rest and refreshing, and revelation.

Chapter 11

The Interpretation of Tongues

To another the interpretation of tongues [by the same Spirit]... (I Corinthians 12:10, NKJV)

In the previous chapter, we covered a misconception in relation to tongues. We covered the definition of tongues by looking at the Greek words used by Paul. We also gave some descriptions for tongues – a secured line and a weapon in spiritual warfare. We also gave the various kinds or classes of tongues that one can experience when tongues is in operation.

In this chapter, I want to speak in regards to the gift of the interpretation of tongues. But before we do that, I want to first make a clear distinction regarding tongues. There is much debate in regards to tongues, and so what I am going to mention requires clarity.

When we discuss the matter of speaking with tongues, there are two types of tongues. Paul, in 1 Corinthians 14, presents this subject of these two types of tongues.

The Two Types of Tongues

In regards to private tongues, this is what you do in the privacy of your devotional time with God. This is you and God communing together. There is no need for interpretation to the public when you are engaged in private tongues. Why? Because, it is private! However, public tongues are messages from God to a worship assembly where there is the need for interpretation in order for everyone to understand what has been uttered. If there is no interpretation, that person spoke presumptuously, and should have remained silent.

We must be careful in public settings with the gift of tongues, because it is a sign and a wonder to unbelievers. It is a gift of God to sinful humanity to confound their proud and haughty minds (1 Corinthians 1:25, 27-31). The purpose of it is to give and leave humanity with a witness that God is calling all men everywhere, all

> **The Two Types of Tongues**
>
> **Private Tongues – tongues used to pray to God, a.k.a. praying in the Spirit**
>
> **Public Tongues - giving a divinely inspired message in tongues to an assembly during corporate worship**

nations and tongues, to repent of their sin. It is a precursor to the Gospel of Jesus Christ when God chooses for it to be used.

However, tongues is not a badge of one's spirituality or spiritual development. The markers for one's spiritual development are:

- Love for God (i.e., obedience; John 14:15, 15:10, 1 John 5:3)
- Love for mankind (i.e., selfless service; John 15:13, Luke 10:29-37)
- Christ-likeness (2 Corinthians 3:17-18, Romans 8:29)

- Renewing of one's mind resulting in transformation (Romans 12:2, Ephesians 4:23)
- The spiritual virtues (Romans 5:3-5, 2 Peter 1:5-9)

Tongues are not a part of this list. It's not a **marker** – revealing the **level** and/or **state** of a believer. On the contrary, it is a **sign** – revealing the **presence** of the Spirit who is within that believer.

Scriptures for Private Tongues

1 Corinthians 14:2, 4, 14, 15, 28

> **For he who speaks in a tongue does not speak to men but to God, for no one understands him; however, in the spirit he speaks mysteries. He who speaks in a tongue edifies himself, but he who prophesies edifies the church. For if I pray in a tongue, my spirit prays, but my understanding is unfruitful. What is the conclusion then? I will pray with the spirit, and I will also pray with the understanding. I will sing with the spirit, and I will also sing with the understanding. But if there is no interpreter, let him keep silent in church, and let him speak to himself and to God.** (NKJV)

Now, let us look at public tongues. Public tongues are just that – public. They are meant for public worship. The function is different. This is tongues where the Spirit-filled believer is not praying or speaking **to** God, but speaking **for** God to others. This is a divinely inspired speech in another language, either known or unknown, to convey the mind and heart of God to a people. This speech **requires** interpretation.

It is a tongue given not for one's own edification, but for the edification of the body gathered for corporate worship. When this tongue is given, it amplifies or magnifies the worship experience, and produces all sorts of blessings to come to the worship service: primarily salvation, then revelation, healing, deliverance, and other experiences.

The question one might pose is "How do I know that God is giving me to speak a message to the corporate body in a worship service?" Prophet Dennis Cramer has been quoted saying "Your public tongues are different from the tongues you speak in your private devotional time." When you have delivered the message, God will grant another its interpretation. If there is not another to give the interpretation, don't fret, God will give you the interpretation as you ask Him for it (1 Corinthians 14:13).

Scripture References for Public Tongues

1 Corinthians 14:13–15, 27, 28

> **Therefore let him who speaks in a tongue pray that he may interpret. For if I pray in a tongue, my spirit prays, but my understanding is unfruitful. What is the conclusion then? I will pray with the spirit, and I will also pray with the understanding. I will sing with the spirit, and I will also sing with the understanding... If anyone speaks in a tongue, let there be two or at the most three, each in turn, and let one interpret. But if there is no interpreter, let him keep silent in church, and let him speak to himself and to God.** (NKJV)

One more thing regarding tongues and its interpretation. When a tongue is given publicly and it is interpreted, it is equal to prophecy. Paul states regarding prophecy:

1 Corinthians 14:5

> **Now I wish that you all spoke in tongues, but even more that you would prophesy; and greater is one who prophesies than one who speaks in tongues, unless he interprets, so that the church may receive edifying.** (NASB)

How to Interpret Tongues

This is the part of this chapter that I want to take the most time in explaining, because it is an aspect that has beleaguered many people in regards to this matter of tongues: how to interpret tongues. When we say interpret, we do not mean translation. The two are different.

The word translation can be defined as the act or process of taking a word, phrase, or sentence from a language and putting it into one's own language by using equivalent words. An example would be taking Spanish words and terms, and exchanging them into English words and terms. Translating is carrying the meaning of what has been said over from one language to another word for word. God may give you a message in tongues that is in Spanish. You don't speak Spanish, but someone in the room does. That message was given, so that person would know that God was the source of the communication, and they need to take to heart what has been said.

Interpretation, on the other hand, can be defined as the act or process of providing the meaning of a word, phrase, sentence, or idea. Interpretation is communicating the idea of what has been spoken supernaturally. Interpretation is when you are receiving the idea or the gist of what has been communicated, and you drape the message in your own words from out of the storehouse of your mind.

In translation, you do not have that freedom. In translation, you have to give it as it was heard in the specific language. If someone is there who speaks the language, and they hear you give the interpretation, when it was supposed to be a translation, it will read in various ways —

1. That your interpretation, if close to the meaning of what was spoken, was accurate, but not the actual rendering verbatim.
2. If the interpretation was off, they will immediately know you made it up. However, interpretation means you receive the gist of the message, and you give its meaning as you understand it.

How It Actually Works

I want to explain the process from giving a message to its interpretation both for private and public tongues. We will begin with private tongues, which actually serves as a means to build up to public tongues.

Interpreting Private Tongues (1 Corinthians 14:13)

As you begin to pray in tongues, you are speaking the appropriate words as given by the Spirit. (Remember, prayer is a conversation with God. Prayer is not a monologue, but a dialogue. God will speak back if you are willing to hear Him.) As you are speaking on this secured line, no other voice can speak except the One who is connected to it, and that being God. While you are talking, you will begin to hear another voice that is likened to a whisper. The voice is small, and at times can be missed. If you are attentive, you will hear His voice. When you begin to hear the voice, be still and listen carefully to what He is saying. Always have a pen and paper handy so as to be able to record what you are receiving (to judge it, because our thoughts can at times muddy the revelation).

Other times, it is like what I am going to share on a personal level & experience in relation to singing in the Spirit.

Singing in the Spirit

1/9/13

This morning, while driving to work, as is my custom, I pray while I drive. I was worshipping the Lord, and began to sing in the Spirit. According to Paul in 1 Corinthians 14:15, you can "sing with the spirit…" (HCSB) The refrain was the same when I got to it, and so I knew that this was a song the Spirit was giving me (1 Chronicles 25:7; 2 Chronicles 29:27).

Then I heard within me, "Sing now in the natural." Paul, in the same verse mentioned above, said we can "sing with the understanding." So, by faith I sang in English. As I began to do so (nervously), I began to receive words in my mind. I listened to the words I sang, and then, I began to realize this was the interpretation of what I sung. As I tried to repeat the words, they were not the exact same words, but they were the same sense or meaning of what the Spirit was singing. The words or interpretation was of my choosing as they came to mind, but they were the words expressing the song the Spirit was giving.

The song was this:

> As I behold our present day
> I see death and sorrow

It causes one to wonder

Where will the world end up tomorrow?

Where will things lead?

But then, I remember the promise of the Lord that I read

That Jesus will crack the sky and return

Rapture us

Taking us away to be with Him.

Then the refrain:

> O Lord, we are waiting for you. O Lord, Your Church is
> waiting for You. (2x)

As I write this now, I'm reminded of the Apostle John's words in
Revelation:

Revelation 22:12, 17, 20

> **"Look! I am coming quickly, and My reward is with
> Me to repay each person according to what he has
> done.... Both the Spirit and the bride say, "Come!"
> Anyone who hears should say, "Come!" And the one
> who is thirsty should come. Whoever desires should
> take the living water as a gift....He who testifies about
> these things says, "Yes, I am coming quickly." Amen!
> Come, Lord Jesus!** (HCSB)

The Spirit was singing this truth and promise to encourage the
Bride of Christ, which I am a part of. The days ahead are difficult
and trying, because of what it states in the following verses.

Revelation 12:12

> **Therefore rejoice, you heavens, and you who dwell in them! Woe to the earth and the sea, for the Devil has come down to you with great fury, because he knows he has a short time.** (HCSB)

Revelation 12:17

> **So the dragon was furious with the woman and left to wage war against the rest of her offspring—those who keep God's commands and have the testimony about Jesus.** (HCSB)

Revelation 6:9-11

> **When He opened the fifth seal, I saw under the altar the people slaughtered because of God's word and the testimony they had. They cried out with a loud voice: "Lord, the One who is holy and true, how long until You judge and avenge our blood from those who live on the earth?" So a white robe was given to each of them, and they were told to rest a little while longer until the number would be completed of their fellow slaves and their brothers, who were going to be killed just as they had been.** (HCSB)

But the promise is that no matter what may come in the future, Christ is with us by his Spirit, and that He will return for us to take us to be with Him forever (Matthew 28:20, Mark 16:20). Simply amazing!

Since then, I have been open to singing in the Spirit more, and getting the interpretation. At times it is a word from the Lord to someone, or to my own self. Most times, the interpretation is worship unto Him, and other times it is revelation in the form of a song. Whatever the message, it is always profound how the Spirit chooses to convey the mind and heart of God.

Interpreting Public Tongues (1 Corinthians 14:5, 27)

Interpretation for public worship is powerful, but many people are fearful to give the meaning of what is said in tongues. The same Spirit that gave the message is the same Spirit that will interpret it. Also remember, it's a message given for the edification of the body (those gathered for worship). The interpretation will bring an enhancement to the service that will catapult everyone into a greater dimension of worship and fellowship with God that has lasting eternal implications. What a powerful opportunity and moment.

So, how do we capture this moment through interpretation in a public tongue? The same way you would a private tongue – by faith. The same way I'm learning to interpret my private devotional tongues is the foundation to interpreting public congregational tongues. All of these grace gifts operate by faith. You cannot operate in the gifts devoid of faith. Faith is the channel by which the gifts find their expression.

Therefore, let us look at some different ways of interpretation.

1. Still small voice
2. Visions
3. Mental pictures
4. Scripture
5. Songs

Each one of these is used by God to give you the interpretation of a tongue. I personally feel the receiving of the interpretation is easier than the giving of the interpretation, but the interpreting part is the more thrilling aspect of it all. Let us deal with each part.

Still Small Voice

As with the private devotional tongue, you can pray in tongues to get the interpretation of what another has spoken as a supernatural message. Yours, of course, will not be audible for all to hear, but it is a way of priming yourself to get the interpretation. It is upon the same wavelength of praying in the Spirit that you will hear His still small voice coming to you granting you the understanding of what He said through the other brother or sister. But, be mindful that what He will say to you in the still small voice will be just the beginnings of the whole. He will not give you the whole. He gives you just enough to get you started in faith. It is as you start with what you heard by the still small voice that more comes (Psalm 81:10). It is like prophesying, because tongues and the interpretation of tongues is equal to prophesying.

Visions

Interpretation comes in the manner of visions. Let me briefly define what a vision is, for many have them and miss the reality of what they are experiencing. Visions are revelations (i.e., supernatural disclosures of spiritual truths and realities in the spiritual realm which affect the natural realm) brought either to one's mind or environment by the Holy Spirit. There are two types of visions: Closed and Open visions. Open visions are supernatural experiences whereby one feels as though they have been transported or the environment has morphed to another setting. Once the vision is over, the setting reverts back to its original state. We will address this a bit further later on in the book when we come to Mental Pictures.

As the person is giving the message in tongues, the Spirit is giving someone a vision of what He is saying. They are either experiencing an open or closed vision. I want to state it here that the length of the message in tongues does not relegate to the length of the interpretation. The interpretation's length is dependent upon the one who is interpreting the vision. If it takes that person a considerable amount of time and words to communicate the meaning of what he has been shown in a vision, then that's how long it takes that person. A note in giving interpretation – you want to give the meat of what God is saying. Follow the principle laid in Scripture as noted in the following verses.

Deuteronomy 4:2

> **You must not add anything to what I command you or take anything away from it, so that you may keep the commands of the LORD your God I am giving you.** (HCSB)

Deuteronomy 12:32

> **You must be careful to do everything I command you; do not add anything to it or take anything away from it.** (HCSB)

Proverbs 30:6

> **Don't add to His words, or He will rebuke you, and you will be proved a liar.** (HCSB)

Romans 12:3, 6

> **For by the grace given to me, I tell everyone among
> you not to think of himself more highly than he should
> think. Instead, think sensibly, as God has distributed a
> measure of faith to each one.... According to the grace
> given to us, we have different gifts: If prophecy, use
> it according to the standard of one's faith...** (HCSB)

Revelation 22:18, 19

> **I testify to everyone who hears the prophetic words
> of this book: If anyone adds to them, God will add to
> him the plagues that are written in this book. And if
> anyone takes away from the words of this prophetic
> book, God will take away his share of the tree of life
> and the holy city, written in this book.** (HCSB)

The principle is do not add nor take away from God's word, but minister it according to the measure of faith afforded you by what the Spirit is either showing or saying to you. Do what the prophet prophesied in his Jeremiah 23:28 as stated in the following verse.

Jeremiah 23:28

> **The prophet who has a dream, let him tell a dream;
> And he who has My word, let him speak My word
> faithfully. What is the chaff to the wheat? says the
> Lord.** (NKJV)

Minister the interpretation of God's supernatural message faithfully, and the benefit as shown in the very next verse will be the result:

Jeremiah 23:29

> **Is not My word like fire [that consumes all that cannot endure the test]? Says the Lord, and like a hammer that breaks in pieces the rock [of most stubborn resistance]?** (AMP)

The word has the power of burning away the dross of false religion, and breaking the rock of stubborn rebellion against God's order. But also, it will ignite the hearts of those whose hearts have grown callous and indifferent, and build the spirits of men who are weak and weary.

Mental Pictures

Mental pictures are likened to closed visions, but they are simply that – pictures to the mind. It is like a still picture, while a closed vision is more active. It is like watching television without sound. You simply see the images, and that's it. Open visions, and there are degrees, are more sensory inclusive. This means that it is not just sight, but you hear, feel/sense, smell, and taste what is occurring within the vision. Closed means restrictive to just the sense of sight, but open means the vision opens up to the other senses of your being.

These mental pictures can be in color or black and white. The more vivid the picture is the more there is within the vision to pick at in which God is conveying. Visions can be 1-dimensional, 2-dimensional, and even 3-dimensional. However, how they come makes no difference. What matters is that you get the gist of what the picture is conveying. Don't get caught up with the pretty lights, but what are the lights saying?

Scripture

Vision Experience

1-dimensional visions = spiritual sight only or mental pictures

2-dimensional visions = other spiritual senses involved: hearing, tasting, smelling, and feeling

3-dimensional visions = interactive – you are literally engaged in the vision by either speech and/or movement (Ezekiel 8; Zechariah 3:1-5)

Here, the Holy Spirit will bring Scripture to your mind. This will bring about a flow of the meaning of what has been divinely communicated. It will most likely be more than one verse. The combination of Scriptures is likened to a collage, and it will give a general understanding of what God is saying. The greater your understanding is of Scripture, the better you are in delivering the interpretation. That is why, it is important to meditate upon God's word day and night (Joshua 1:8, Psalm 1:1-3). One's success in the supernatural hinges upon one's possession of Scripture. Are you hiding God's word in your heart through daily meditation (Psalm 119:11)?

Songs

Sometimes, God will use a known song to convey the meaning of the message given. You do not need to sing the interpretation, but take the lyrics and use them as your inspiration. The lyrics will have the anointing or glory of God upon them as you speak them at that moment to that specific group of believers. It is God's word to them. Not only that, but the familiarity of the song will then stick with the people, and it will serve as a constant reminder from that day God had spoken to them. Also, at the moment when you have finished giving the interpretation, the Spirit may then lead everyone to sing the very song that was used as a means of interpretation. What was a message became the foundation for worship. What a way to see John 4:24, **"worship in spirit and truth"**. (HCSB)

There may be more ways that the interpretation may come, but these are the one's God would have me to share in this book at this time. The more you are exposed to this reality, the more you become daring with your faith, the more you long to be a blessing to the Body of Christ, and the more God will grant you the means to interpret tongues.

A Note of Caution

Many people, due to an inordinate sense of self confidence, have sought to use the gifts as a means to promote and advance themselves. Even where it relates to the gift of interpretation of tongues. The gifts are for the purpose of edifying the Body of Christ, but unfortunately, they were used to build the individual's ego & kingdom.

We must check our hearts at the threshold of worship. We must not allow false worship and strange fire to corrupt our service to God simply because of a selfish desire of wanting to be seen and to make a name for ourselves. Worship is not about ourselves, but about the God who has saved us from the evil perils of sin, Satan, and the grave.

If there is a message given in tongues, there are some things that we must establish before we get up to give its interpretation. The first thing is, recognize the atmosphere. Worship is the by-product of thanksgiving and praise. Worship happens when the glory of God is within a place, and there are degrees or levels to the glory. The greatest or highest aspect to this is when the glory fills a place and is in a tangible form. This is called Shekinah. When that degree of His glory is within a place, human led worship takes a back seat. The glory charged atmosphere is the leading reality within that place, and it is what leads, guides, and inspires the worship. Everyone is experiencing the wonder of His presence. There is a unity borne of the Spirit whereby everyone is operating in sync. No one is off doing their own thing, but everyone is in an order – the order of the Spirit. No one is the leader, but One – the Holy Spirit.

Thanksgiving and praise is the precursor to worship. What this means is that they create this reality of the glory of God. In the Old Testament, the priest was responsible to offer sacrifices unto the Lord. We see the inauguration of the tabernacle and priestly ministry, Aaron offers the sacrifice, and the fire of the Lord came from heaven and consumed the sacrifice. This was an Old Testament prelude of what the New Testament saint would do spiritually. What they did physically is what we do spiritually. The results are still the same – the manifestation of the glory of God.

One can expect these following signs:

1. Spiritual fire descending from heaven (Acts 1:1-4).
2. Breakthroughs in the heavenly realm where demonic powers are oppressively dominant and controlling of terrestrial space (Joel 2:30).
3. Freedom from demonic oppression: spiritual, mental, emotional, and/or physical.
4. The release of spiritual language and communication from heaven.
5. The preservation of life from outward natural dangers and poisonous evils.
6. The healing of bodies from all forms of ailments.

We have covered in this chapter the gift of the interpretation of tongues, and we have covered the nine gifts of the Spirit in these last few eleven chapters.

Now, in the following chapters, we will cover how to operate in the gifts. Chapter 13 will help show how to stir the gifts in you, so that they can have their expression through you as you yield yourself to the Holy Spirit.

SUMMARY

The gift of the interpretation of tongues:

1. Is a gift in which the same Spirit that gave the message is the same Spirit that will interpret it.
2. Is not translating a language, for in translation, you are carrying the meaning of what has been said word for word.
3. Is giving the meaning of what has been said in one's own words; communicating the idea of what has been spoken supernaturally.
4. Is a gift for the purpose of edifying (i.e., building up) the Body of Christ.

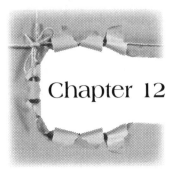

Chapter 12

How to Operate in the Gifts of the Spirit

But solid food is for the mature—for those whose senses have been trained to distinguish between good and evil. (Hebrews 5:14, HCSB)

As we have come to this point of the study on the gifts of the Spirit as recorded in 1 Corinthians 12, I want to begin by dealing with a few misconceptions. These misconceptions are hindrances to the believer in operating in the gifts. If one can come to a place of proper understanding, it will free one whereby the gifts will flow with such ease and freedom. For Paul states, **"Now the Lord is the Spirit, and where the Spirit of the Lord is, there is liberty."** (2 Corinthians 3:17, NASB) Liberty is one of the hallmarks of the Holy Spirit. Satan is the one who endeavors to bind, confine, limit, and oppress, for Paul writes in Romans 8:15, **"For [the Spirit which] you have now received [is] not a spirit of slavery to put you once more in bondage..."** (AMP)

As we look at each one of these misconceptions, the Holy Spirit is pulling the limits off. He is realigning our understanding with the spiritual reality of what Christ has afforded us for effectual ministry whereby Satan's kingdom can be pulled down and toppled. Let us now take a look at each one of these misconceptions.

Ultra-Holiness

The first misconception is that in order for one to operate in the gifts of the Spirit, you must be an ultra-holy person. This is a person who holds to an extreme perspective on holiness. Now, holiness is a concept that is misunderstood by many. Holiness to some is simply a legalistic outward show of religiosity. It has the appearance of conformity, but devoid of transformation that is inward & progressive. Others perceive holiness as sinless-ness. For those who are persuaded by such a belief, they feel that they are not "holy enough" to operate in the gifts due to some sin in their life.

This misconception fails to take note of what Christ did at the cross. What He accomplished at the cross is sufficient for us to operate in the gifts of the Spirit. The gifts of the Spirit are grace gifts. They are not given upon the merit of the individual, but based upon the sacrifice of Christ and the faithfulness of God to His own Word. The word of God states that we were made holy by the blood of Christ (Hebrews 9:14, 10:29). We are already holy, for His blood is enough!

Acts 3:12

> **So when Peter saw it, he responded to the people: "Men of Israel, why do you marvel at this? Or why look so intently at us, as though by our own power or godliness (i.e., holiness) we had made this man walk? (NKJV)**

I must qualify this aspect of holiness. Though we are holy from the point of the new birth, we are called to grow within and from that holiness. Holiness is a Christian character that is to be developed. Our character serves as a cap on our gifting, and we can only develop in our gifting per the level of our character. You cannot increase beyond your character, for the gifts operate in relation to Christian virtues (Galatians 5:22-23; 2 Peter 1:2-11). There is much to teach on this aspect, which I do not have the space to treat within this volume.

Lots of Faith

The next misconception is that we need to have a lot of faith to operate in the gifts of the Spirit. Listen to a conversation the disciples had with Jesus regarding this very matter in the following verses.

Luke 17:5, 6

> **The apostles said to the Lord, "Increase our faith." "If you have faith the size of a mustard seed," the Lord said, "you can say to this mulberry tree, 'Be uprooted and planted in the sea,' and it will obey you."** (HCSB)

They saw what Jesus did in expelling the demon, and they thought to themselves if they were to do the very same thing, it would require them to have an increased amount of faith. Christ corrected their understanding of faith. They thought, "We need a lot of faith to do these kinds of works." However, Christ stated what they needed was genuine quality of faith. It can be small, but it will be sufficient to get the job done.

You do not need a lot of faith to operate in the gifts of the Spirit. Faith is likened to a pipe in which the grace of God can funnel through (Ephesians 2:8). The size of the pipe will determine how fast and how much the amount of grace can flow through. But regardless of the size or measure, the grace will flow. So, stop waiting for a bigger size pipe of faith, and work with the size you have now. You will be surprised by what God can accomplish.

Fasting

The next misconception is that one must fast a lot in order to operate in the gifts of the Spirit. The reasoning behind this is that fasting augments the anointing or gifting in your life. Where do we get this notion?

Luke 4:1-2

> **Then Jesus returned from the Jordan, full of the Holy Spirit, and was led by the Spirit in the wilderness for 40 days to be tempted by the Devil. He ate nothing during those days, and when they were over, He was hungry.** (HCSB)

Luke 4:14

> **Then Jesus returned to Galilee in the power of the Spirit, and news about Him spread throughout the entire vicinity.** (HCSB)

We see in these few verses that Jesus was led into the wilderness, and during that time He fasted. In verse 18, we see the result of that time – power! Now, in order for us to get the proper understanding of what is happening here, we have to look at Jesus' words.

Luke 4:18

> **The Spirit of the Lord is on Me, because He has anointed Me to preach good news to the poor. He**

has sent Me to proclaim freedom to the captives and recovery of sight to the blind, to set free the oppressed, to proclaim the year of the Lord's favor. (HCSB)

Acts 1:8

But you will receive power when the Holy Spirit has come on you, and you will be My witnesses in Jerusalem, in all Judea and Samaria, and to the ends of the earth." (HCSB)

In essence, Jesus shows us here that when we receive the baptism with the Holy Spirit, we are anointed with power. We receive God's empowerment to operate in the gifts of the Spirit. Consequently, when Jesus was filled with the Spirit, He received power. However, that power simply resided within Him. In order for the power to go from Him, there needed to be a way out for it – brokenness! Therefore, fasting is not for gifting, but for the breaking of the outward man. We will deal with this more a bit later in chapter thirteen.

Maturity

The next misconception is that in order for you to operate in the gifts, you need to be mature. Thus, the gifts are not for novices. Where is this taken from? Many get this from Paul's words to Timothy, his son in the faith. Let us look at the text.

1 Timothy 3:1-4, 6, 7

This saying is trustworthy: "If anyone aspires to be an overseer, he desires a noble work." An overseer, therefore, must be above reproach, the husband of one

wife, self-controlled, sensible, respectable, hospitable, an able teacher, not addicted to wine, not a bully but gentle, not quarrelsome, not greedy— one who manages his own household competently, having his children under control with all dignity...He must not be a new convert, or he might become conceited and fall into the condemnation of the Devil. Furthermore, he must have a good reputation among outsiders, so that he does not fall into disgrace and the Devil's trap. (HCSB)

This portion of Scripture is not dealing with the matter of the gifts of the Spirit, but in relation to a ministry gift or office of leadership within the Church. If someone desires to be a leader, he must not be a new convert to the faith. Again, this is not regarding the gifts, but in regards to leadership.

In relation to the gifts, there is no requirement for maturity. A new convert can receive the baptism with the Holy Spirit. They do not necessarily need to spend a long time waiting to be filled, nor after being filled to operate in the gifts. We are the ones who prolong the steps, and by virtue of that cause people to falter into religion rather than the spiritual heritage of those who are followers of Christ. The gifts function by virtue of grace, not of works of piety or of a period of development. The gifts are not a sign of maturity, but an affirmation of the resurrected Christ and a manifestation of the Holy Spirit.

The gifts do not require you to be perfect, for they are a reflection of the perfections of Christ by means and virtue of the Holy Spirit. Thus, when the gifts are in operation, they reveal the perfections of His glory! They may cause your imperfections to be seen, but people will be so enamored by the greatness of His perfection that they will be moved to receive Him. Why? Because, if God being perfect can use you an imperfect person, truly He is worthy of worship and obedience.

To summarize this chapter, I would like to use Dr. Bill Hamon's quote from his book entitled *The Day of the Saints*:

> "Gifts are manifested by those who receive, believe, and demonstrate regardless of their personal imperfections, failures, and immaturity...The ideal is gifts operating from the fruit of the Spirit and godly character. (pg. 317-318)"

These are the misconceptions that God has granted me to learn and see over these years, but what are the things then that are needful for us to operate in the gifts of the Spirit? In the next chapter, we will begin to see what those things are. We will first deal with the needful things, and then move to discuss the helpful things that help stir and cultivate the gifts.

Chapter 13

How to Operate in the Gifts of the Spirit

But solid food is for full-grown men, for those whose senses and mental faculties are trained by practice to discriminate and distinguish between what is morally good and noble and what is evil and contrary to divine or human law. (Hebrews 5:14, AMP)

In the last chapter, we looked at the misconceptions that some people have in regards to the gifts of the Spirit: ultra-holiness, lots of faith, fasting, and maturity. Now we want to look at what we need to have in order to function in the gifts. I am going to deal with this aspect by layers, and the first layer is Spiritual Foundations. The second layer is Spiritual Graces, and the last layer is Spiritual Devotions.

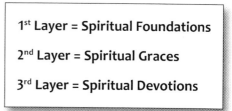

1st Layer = Spiritual Foundations

2nd Layer = Spiritual Graces

3rd Layer = Spiritual Devotions

Spiritual Foundations

Let us begin with the first layer. In Spiritual Foundations, there are only two needful principles that are required in order to operate in the gifts:

1. Be Born Again – John 3:3, 5
2. Be Baptized with the Holy Spirit – Acts 19:6

Both are the sovereign work of God that is received by those who repent and place their faith in Jesus Christ as Lord, Savior, and Baptizer with the Holy Spirit.

Why must one be born again? The reason is a person must have a new nature conducive to the Holy Spirit. Prior to the new birth experience, we were led by another spirit – the spirit of this world (1 Corinthians 2:12, 12:2, Ephesians 2:2). Our sinful nature was conducive to that spirit. Now that we are in Christ, we have a new nature and we must live, operate, and be led by a new spirit (Ezekiel 11:19, 18:31, 36:26).

Also, the blood of Christ plays a pivotal role. The blood of Christ is how sin is purged from one's life. Look at the following verses, and see a brief overview of what the blood accomplishes.

Hebrews 9:14

> **How much more will the blood of the Messiah, who through the eternal Spirit offered Himself without blemish to God, cleanse our consciences from dead works to serve the living God?** (HCSB)

Hebrews 9:22

> **In fact, according to the Law of Moses, nearly everything was purified with blood. For without the shedding of blood, there is no forgiveness.** (NLT)

1 John 1:7, 9

> **But if we walk in the light, as he is in the light, we have fellowship with one another, and the blood of Jesus, his Son, purifies us from all sin...If we confess our sins, he is faithful and just and will forgive us our sins and purify us from all unrighteousness.** (NIV)

Christ bore our sins, shed His blood, so that His sacrifice would obtain for us forgiveness of sin. The blood which ran from His veins cleanses away those sins. The blood also cleanses our consciences, which deals with guilt and shame. Furthermore, the blood redeems our bodies from the enemy (1 Corinthians 6:20, Revelation 5:9). In spirit, soul, and body, we are made holy, so that we can be made fit to be recipients of His Holy Spirit. We were made holy persons to receive a Holy Person.

The baptism with the Holy Spirit is not simply the reception of power, but the reception of a Person who comes to live within us on a permanent basis. He does not come empty handed, but He brings His authority and power. Furthermore, He brings gifts as did Abraham's servant to Rebekah (Genesis 24:22, 30, 53), who was the soon to be bride of Abraham's son Isaac. Therefore, the Holy Spirit is a servant who comes according to the will of God bearing gifts to impart inwardly where the end result will be an outward demonstration of God's power in relation to the promise, resurrected, and exalted Son Jesus. The gifts are not accessories to the believer, so that he or she may parade about proving his or her spirituality, but they are tools and weapons granted for the sake of effective kingdom ministry and kingdom warfare. They are part of our inheritance for which Christ died, so that we may use them to advance His kingdom in the earth.

These are the two things that we need: **be born again** and **be baptized with the Holy Spirit**. If you have been born again and are baptized, then you are positioned to operate in the gifts of the Holy Spirit.

Spiritual Graces

Having established these two very important foundational principles, let us move onto four major aspects that serve as the heart of the believer in regards to the supernatural: **grace**, **faith**, **hope**, and **love**. These four things make it possible for us to function in the supernatural. These things are necessities if one desires to operate in the gifts and to move in greater levels of effectiveness (1 Corinthians 1:7, AMP).

In a previous chapter, I dealt with this aspect of God's grace, but I want to delve a bit further, so as to give a better understanding regarding the importance of God's grace. For if we understand the grace of God, it will revolutionize the way we approach the subject of the gifts, and help us to be free in operating in them.

The word grace means "unmerited favor". We have established this aspect before, but another aspect to **the grace of God is that it is the power of the Holy Spirit** (James 4:6, AMP). It is a power that is immeasurable. Thus, the grace of God is limitless or beyond measure (Romans 5:15, 20, AMP).

Galatians 3:5

> **So then, does God supply you with the Spirit and work miracles among you by the works of the law or by hearing with faith?** (HCSB)

The Spirit is the agent of God's grace (Zechariah 12:10). He is the One who administers the grace or power of God to produce the miraculous amongst us. Notice the rendering of the words and the connection between them: "Spirit to you" and "miracles among you". The "you" helps us to see what God is trying to convey to us about the supernatural. God supplies the Spirit to us, and the Spirit works the miracles among us. The linking factor is one major thing – receiving! How we receive and yield to the Spirit will determine how much of His activity we make room for. We shall see this principle in the next few verses.

Isaiah 59:16

> **And He saw that there was no man and wondered that there was no intercessor [no one to intervene on behalf of truth and right]; therefore His own arm brought Him victory, and His own righteousness [having the Spirit without measure] sustained Him.** (AMP)

John 3:34

> **For since He Whom God has sent speaks the words of God [proclaims God's own message], God does not give Him His Spirit sparingly or by measure, but boundless is the gift God makes of His Spirit! [Deut. 18:18.]** (AMP)

Notice how both references refer to Jesus having received the Spirit without measure. The grace of God (i.e., the ministry of the Spirit in power) is boundless, and Christ received Him in that manner. There was no limitation from the point of Christ where it related to the Holy Spirit. When the Spirit went to give forth His power, His power was not met with any measure that would limit it. Thus, great miracles, signs and wonders, and gifts of the Spirit would happen freely and regularly. Why? He received the Spirit without measure!

The question lies then, how do we receive the grace of God? How do we receive the ministry of the Holy Spirit in power? The next verse will show us how.

Ephesians 2:8, 9

> **For you are saved by grace through faith, and this is not from yourselves; it is God's gift— not from works, so that no one can boast.** (HCSB)

The way we receive is by faith! But for us to understand how we operate by what we receive is by understanding how faith is seen biblically.

Romans 12:3

> **For through the grace given to me I say to everyone among you not to think more highly of himself than he ought to think; but to think so as to have sound judgment, as God has allotted to each a measure of faith.** (NASB)

While grace is measureless, faith on the other hand is by measure. Each of us have received grace and faith. We have been afforded the access to unlimited power, but the means by which this power operates within or through is a limited means. As shared before using a different illustration, grace is likened to an ocean, and you're seeking to pass the ocean through a straw. That is a difficult means, but God chooses to operate through such means. Why?

Again, the way I have come to understand faith and how I define it is "**faith is <u>conviction</u> in the identity of God and <u>confidence</u> in the ability of God**". You cannot be confident in God's ability if you do not possess an intimate rooted knowledge of His identity. How does one gain this knowledge? One is able to gain such knowledge of His identity through continuous meditation upon the Word of God (Deuteronomy 8:3, Matthew 4:4, Luke 4:4)! Furthermore, His identity revealed by the Word is the foundation for one's confidence in what God says He can and will do. Therefore, when we step out by what we have heard from the Spirit, that step denotes faith in His ability to manifest the gifts of His choosing to accomplish the task set before you. **The more you walk in the Spirit, walking by His guidance or promptings (as varied as they are), the more faith you build allowing for a greater and quicker expression of His power in and through you**.

The next thing I want to cover is the aspect of hope. Hope stems from faith.

Hebrews 11:1

> **Now faith is the substance of things hoped for, the evidence of things not seen.** (NKJV)

Faith is not faith devoid of hope. Why? Because in faith, what you are saying is that you are confident in God's ability to perform what He said He could do and would do. Therefore, you move in expectation as the Holy Spirit guides you through the various means that He chooses to prompt you into action, so He can act in accordance to the will of God.

Hope is expectation to one's faith. If one does not expect to see anything, then one does not believe. You may doubt, but if you move, your faith is greater than your doubt. The more you move in the Spirit, the greater your faith becomes, and the larger the medium of your faith is for the Spirit to operate and manifest Himself by way of the gifts. This is how Jesus could do the things He demonstrated. The grace of God, by the agency of the Holy Spirit, through His faith (which did not have any doubt or unbelief, because He knew the Father intimately) with the evidence of His hope in God brought about by the manifestation of the Spirit's power to manifest the gifts. Your faith grows as you walk or obey by becoming ever sensitive and willing to obey, and obeying when you receive His prompting. You will see the Spirit do amazing things!

The last aspect or principle is the greatest of them all. I don't give this opinion of my own, but the apostle Paul himself writes that this is the greatest – love!

1 Corinthians 12:31

> **But earnestly desire the best gifts. And yet I show you a more excellent way.** (NKJV)

1 Corinthians 13:13

> **And now abide faith, hope, love, these three; but the greatest of these is love.** (NKJV)

The more excellent way of operating in the gifts is by the way of love. Why and how is that?

Let me begin with a definition of love inspired by the cannon of Scripture. **Love is the pursuit of the welfare and gratification of another dependent upon God at the expense of oneself.** The following verses are the matrix of such a definition.

John 3:16

> **"For God so loved the world that He gave His only begotten Son, that whoever believes in Him shall not perish, but have eternal life.** (NASB)

John 15:13-14

> **No one has greater love than this, that someone would lay down his life for his friends. You are My friends if you do what I command you.** (HCSB)

1 John 3:16

> **This is how we have come to know love: He laid down His life for us. We should also lay down our lives for our brothers.** (HCSB)

As you see in the John 3:16 passage, because of God's love for humanity, the Godhead worked to bring about the salvation of men. The rebirth is a supernatural miracle. It is the greatest miracle! It is a sign or evidence of the hidden person of the Spirit, for He is the agent that brings about the rebirth experience. Furthermore, it is a wonder, because to see how someone such as the apostle Paul once was a persecutor to now being one willing to die for the sake of Christ is amazing.

With that understanding, the gifts work best by way of love, because love is the heart beat of God. Matter of fact, God is love (1

John 4:8, 16)! Therefore, when you operate in love, you are tapping into God's person & power.

Love serves as the means of giving one a target – the other person. The goal is not oneself, but others. Operating in the gifts is an "other person" oriented thing. It is selfless. To effectively function in the gifts, one must become "other oriented" if he is to ever hit the mark of glorifying God, edifying the other believer who is the recipient of such supernatural ministry, and salvation of those who are lost in their sins.

Love is the means of connecting the drive within the heart to move one to serve another God's grace, and the goal marker for the believer so he or she always hits the target. That is why Paul says without love, you are nothing! Without love, you will miss every time.

Now, let us move to the next layer to help solidify how to operate in the gifts of the Spirit.

Grace through Faith	Faith (← Hope) through Love
Ephesians 2:8	Galatians 5:6

|	|

Expectation	→	Manifestation

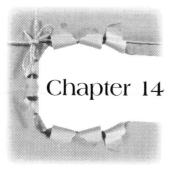

Chapter 14

How to Operate in the Gifts of the Spirit

Solid food is for those who are mature, who through training have the skill to recognize the difference between right and wrong. (Hebrews 5:14, NLT)

We have come to the final part of how to operate in the gifts of the Spirit. We have looked at the first layer being Spiritual Foundations – be born again and be baptized with the Spirit. We then looked at the next layer being Spiritual Graces: grace, faith, hope, and the greatest being love. Now, we are going to look at the final layer being Spiritual Devotions that help us operate in the gifts of the Spirit.

Spiritual Devotions

There are many things that we can pull on to teach regarding this aspect of this layer, but the ones I want to stress are the ones that have helped me greatly.

Meditation

I want to first begin with meditation upon the word of God. Why meditation upon the Word in relation to the gifts? The reason being is because the Word is foundational to all we do. In a kingdom, a king's word is law. God rules over His people as a King by virtue of His Word, for His Word is the rule of the kingdom.

Ecclesiastes 8:4

> **For the king's word is authoritative, and who can say to him, "What are you doing?"** (HCSB)

To understand the importance of the Word, we have to look at what Scripture teaches regarding the Word.

Hebrews 4:12

> **For the Word that God speaks is alive and full of power [making it active, operative, energizing, and effective]; it is sharper than any two-edged sword, penetrating to the dividing line of the breath of life (soul) and [the immortal] spirit, and of joints and marrow [of the deepest parts of our nature], exposing and sifting and analyzing and judging the very thoughts and purposes of the heart.** (AMP)

Several things the author of Hebrews reveals about the Word of God:

1. It is alive [full of divine life].
2. It is full of [divine] power.
3. It is sharp, meaning it is [deeply] penetrating.

4. It is a discerner, meaning it makes accurate judgments regarding the mind and heart of a person.

This is the power of the Word of God, and it becomes the basis for our lives. Not only our lives, but the ministry we render to one another and the world. Without the Word, we are vulnerable and susceptible to all manner of erroneous beliefs and practices that are lifeless and fruitless, and which shipwreck our faith and derail our ministry.

Romans 10:17

So then faith comes by hearing, and hearing by the word of God. (NKJV)

Another important factor to note regarding the Word is that it is the means by which faith comes to the human heart. When we actively and repetitively hear the word of God, it causes faith to be conceived whereby what will be birthed is the manifestation of that word. The more we immerse ourselves in Scripture regarding the supernatural, the more faith we come to have as an avenue for the Spirit to manifest Himself by the gifts.

Romans 12:2

Do not be conformed to this age, but be transformed by the renewing of your mind, so that you may discern what is the good, pleasing, and perfect will of God. (HCSB)

The next thing you must seize is the importance of daily meditation upon the Word. When you meditate upon the Word, what you are doing is transplanting your mind from the soil of this culture and replanting it within the soil of the kingdom of heaven.

You are going from this world's system to the system of God. You are going from worldly thinking to kingdom thinking, and kingdom thinking is not anything related to this world. Kingdom thinking is thinking far above and far superior to this world's way of reasoning.

This is critical, because what the mind has to have in order to operate in the gifts requires a mind that is heavenly. Paul calls this "being spiritually minded" (Romans 8:6). This sort of mind is one that is under the guidance and influence of the Holy Spirit. How does the Holy Spirit guide and influence the mind? By virtue of the Word! As you continually dwell in the Word, He destroys the previous strongholds (i.e., the previously held mental paradigms that were anti-God and anti-Christ), and He rebuilds a new stronghold (i.e., a new mental paradigm or structural frame by which to function out of, which is in harmony with God/Christ) conducive to effective supernatural ministry, which is under the jurisdiction of the kingdom of God.

If your mind is not renewed daily, operating in the gifts will be difficult, because there are principles that must be grasped and the carnal mind cannot grasp them. Also, the Holy Spirit will lead you in ways that are contrary to natural thinking, but the results are supernaturally borne. Renewing the mind through daily meditation is another way of seeing the mind under reconstruction to build an edifice whereby the Spirit of God can dwell in a sanctified temple, which we are (2 Corinthians 6:14).

Praying in the Spirit

Jude 1:20

> **But you, beloved, build yourselves up [founded] on your most holy faith [make progress, rise like an edifice higher and higher], praying in the Holy Spirit...** (AMP)

Praying in the Holy Spirit, is a powerful devotional activity that some believers do not quite understand in regards to its significance and role in the Christian's arsenal or weaponry. Amidst the many things that can be said about tongues, the one thing I want to say here is that tongues edifies the one praying.

The Greek word found here in Jude for edify is oikodomeō (Strong's Concordance #3618), and it means "to build up". Thus, the implication of the word means "to improve (to turn something into profit) spiritually". When you pray in tongues, you are bringing yourself into a more desirable condition or state. Thus, to edify means to make the spirit more useful, profitable, and advantageous.

The word edify is a construction term. You are building an edifice, or a massive structure that reaches upward. What is it that you are building? You are building the spirit man. Praying in tongues is the language of the human spirit in direct communication with God. Therefore, it is solely the operation or activity of the spirit man. The soul simply waits on the sidelines until it is beckoned by the spirit to give the soul orders derived from communion with God. Therefore, as you pray in tongues, the spirit is being built up. It is being fortified in its supremacy in relation to the other parts of the human personality.

Also, when you pray in tongues, you are going up higher in the Spirit. What I mean by this is that you are getting closer to God whereby your level of sensitivity and discernment is greater, and there is less carnal influence by means of your flesh (i.e., lower nature). So, praying in tongues affords you a greater level of sensitivity to the realm of the spirit.

Another powerful key that I have found to unlocking the gifts of the Spirit in regards to praying in tongues is that it is one of the fastest ways to get into the Spirit (2 Timothy 1:6). When you pray in tongues, you directly engage the spirit man. The more that you engage your spirit man on purpose, the more active that part of you will be under the guidance and power of the Spirit of God.

When you pray in tongues, Paul states something that every Spirit-filled believer needs to establish within themselves.

1 Corinthians 14:14

> **For if I pray in a tongue, my spirit prays, but my understanding is unfruitful.** (NKJV)

> **If I pray in tongues, my spirit prays but my mind lies fallow, and all that intelligence is wasted.** (MSG)

> **For if I pray in tongues, my spirit is praying, but I don't understand what I am saying.** (NLT)

I want to establish this point again for repetition's sake – praying in tongues is the activity of the spirit man under the guidance and power of the Spirit of God. The mind, which is a division of the soul, is unfruitful, does nothing, cannot understand, and too many, feel that their intelligence is wasted. Oh how far that is from the truth!

The soul may be inactive and unable to understand, but as mentioned before, it is a servant awaiting orders. Isaiah said, **"But they that wait upon the LORD shall renew their strength..."** (40:31 KJV) The understanding of wait is the term for a servant. Just like a waiter or waitress waiting on tables. Though not able to understand the thoughts of the patron, they wait attentively for the order. When the order comes, it is the revelation of the longing within the mind of the patron. This longing is the verbalized order in understood language to the servant, and the servant quickly goes to fulfill the order. This going is what strengthens the servant, and each and every time an order is given, it brings with it new impetus and drive. A true servant finds fulfillment and strength in service.

This is what the soul goes through. It waits like a servant longing patiently to receive orders that are revealed by the Spirit to the mind. The revelation will come in all types of forms. The believer must not mentally disengage when praying in tongues, but actively discern what the Holy Spirit will submit to his or her mind. Sometimes, the revelation will come in the form of a Scripture. Other times, a familiar song. At times, the revelation will come as words written across the mind. The list could go on and on. The key thing to grasp is do not go to sleep just because you are praying in tongues, but be mentally engaged by waiting. When you do so, you will be able to vocalize what God is saying and doing.

Worship

This then serves as a great segue to speak in regards to the next devotional being worship.

> **But those who wait for the Lord [who expect, look for, and hope in Him] shall change and renew their strength and power; they shall lift their wings and mount up [close to God] as eagles [mount up to the sun]; they shall run and not be weary, they shall walk and not faint or become tired. (AMP)**

As we saw in the last devotional, we can see that waiting upon the Lord opens one to be a channel of power in relation to the Holy Spirit and the gifts, but also it yields great results as seen here in the Isaiah 40:31 text – boundless strength where a Spirit-filled believer will go on and on without running out of steam.

As an example, in relation to prophesying. I have felt at times like prophesying to everyone within a meeting. One such service, I sought to prophesy to as many as I could, and as I did, the anointing seemed to increase and increase. It did not decrease through use, but grew in dimension, scope, power, and effect (Luke 6:38). Why did that occur, and how to capitalize on that reality regularly? In part, waiting upon the Lord!

Now let me help you to understand further what I mean by waiting upon the Lord through a few Scripture references as shown in these following verses.

Luke 24:49

> **Behold, I send the Promise of My Father upon you; but tarry in the city of Jerusalem until you are endued with power from on high."** (NKJV)

Here Jesus commands the apostles and other believers to wait in Jerusalem for the Holy Spirit, for they would receive His power to be able to go forth to evangelize the world, and making disciples of all the nations. How did they interpret waiting?

Luke 24:51-53

> **Now it came to pass, while He blessed them, that He was parted from them and carried up into heaven. And they worshiped Him, and returned to Jerusalem with great joy, and were continually in the temple praising and blessing God. Amen.** (NKJV)

They interpreted waiting as continuous worship.

David says in Psalms 84:1-2, 4:

> **How lovely is Your tabernacle, O LORD of hosts! My soul longs, yes, even faints for the courts of the LORD; My heart and my flesh cry out for the living God...Blessed are those who dwell in Your house; they will still be praising You. Selah** (NKJV)

He also says something to note in Psalms 92:13:

> **Those who are planted in the house of the LORD shall flourish in the courts of our God.** (NKJV)

Being planted means you are fixed and cannot (i.e., will not) move. Your roots are in the soil of where you are planted. David reveals what soil this is which we are called to be planted within – the house of the Lord. The house represents here as the presence of God. When we are planted in the presence of the Lord, we flourish or break out of the limitations of this realm, and bud forth the realities of the realm of the courts of God. We go from one court to another experiencing the wonders of His presence, His judicial orders that impact the realities on planet earth below, and we walk in His dominion as His representatives on earth causing His kingdom decrees to be realities as we express and endeavor to fulfill His kingdom will on earth as it is in heaven resulting in its advancement.

Waiting upon the Lord is powerfully important, and the way we do so is by worshipping Him. The gifts come alive in an atmosphere of habitual worship. Sean Smith states in *Prophetic Evangelism*, "The prophetic is an anointing for revelatory release and a spiritual flow that we must contend for 24/7," and how true is his statement! (pg. 61) Being a worshipper is powerfully purposeful. When you understand the purpose of a thing, you then can do it on purpose to produce its results. God is seeking for a people who will worship Him to bring about the results of the gifts of the Spirit on purpose twenty four seven (John 4:23).

Let us look at two references where worship creates an atmosphere where the gifts come alive and are the result.

2 Kings 3:14-15

> **And Elisha said, "As the LORD of hosts lives, before whom I stand, surely were it not that I regard the presence of Jehoshaphat king of Judah, I would not look at you, nor see you. But now bring me a musician." Then it happened, when the musician played, that the hand of the LORD came upon him.** (NKJV)

Acts 13:2

> **While they were worshiping the Lord and fasting, the Holy Spirit said, separate now for Me Barnabas and Saul for the work to which I have called them.** (AMP)

In both references, we see that worship was the means by which to connect with the supernatural realm of God whereby God moved by His Spirit to influence his servants to speak prophetically the will and purpose of God. Again, the gifts come alive in an atmosphere of worship. When you are a worshipper, a person who lives by ministering to the Lord regularly as do the angels, then you will have the reality of His presence and glory in your life. Accordingly, ministry by the gifts will not be laborious, but there will be a liberty and freedom that you have not known previously. This is how you also cultivate the prophetic in your life.

John 4:23

> **But an hour is coming, and is now here, when the true worshipers will worship the Father in spirit and truth. Yes, the Father wants such people to worship Him.** (HCSB)

This is the hour for the people of God to position themselves as Anna, who the Bible says **"did not depart from the temple, but served God with fastings and prayers night and day."** (Luke 2:37 NKJV) This prophetess, because she lived in this manner, was privileged to see before her death the Lord Jesus when He came into the temple. As a result, she spoke to all about Him that came into the temple. Worship will position us to see things about the Lord, and be able to communicate those things about Him to His people. Worshippers are afforded insight into the kingdom of heaven than any other person, because they have the intentions of the King's heart as their priority (1 Samuel 13:14).

Fasting

I now want to cover this next devotional, which is fasting. Fasting is a powerful yet misunderstood devotion, and I encourage all to read Derek Prince's book entitled *Shaping History through Prayer and Fasting.* I also advise all to peruse Pastor Jentezen Franklin's resources on fasting: *Fasting 101: Fasting Basics, Fasting 2.0: Next Level, and Fasting in the Footsteps of Jesus.* One can find these resources on his webpage: www.JentezenFranklin.org/fasting/. These resource materials on fasting will be life transforming.

The question that we must ask ourselves is "What does fasting have to do with the gifts?" First of all, I've learned that fasting does not do anything for your gifting. It does not directly impact it, but it does impact it indirectly. What I mean is that fasting does not target your gift, but something else that will help promote the gifts in you. To understand, we will turn to David's words in the Psalms.

Psalm 69:10

> **When I wept, and chastened my soul with fasting, that was to my reproach.** (KJV)

> **Fasting targets your flesh.**

The evidence of fasting is seen throughout Scripture, and it is a powerful spiritual exercise. Some of the benefits of fasting are captured in Isaiah 58. To reiterate, however, fasting does nothing for the gifts. The gifts do not need help, for they are perfect as the One who gave them out of the resource of His person or essence. Thus, fasting will not make the gifts more powerful or less powerful due to the lack thereof of fasting. Again, fasting does not target the gifts, but what it does target is your flesh!

In the verse referenced above, David states he chastened his soul with fasting. Therefore, **fasting is a means or method of disciplining the soul to come under submission to God and the spirit of man.** It helps to break the will of the sinful nature whereby you come to be yielded to the Spirit's will. It is the breaking of the outer man to bring about the life and power of what is contained in the inner man. I encourage the reader to also read Watchman Knee's book entitled *The Breaking of the Outer Man and the Release of the Spirit.*

Isaiah states in chapter 58 something powerful to note.

Isaiah 58:6, 8

> **"Is this not the fast that I have chosen: to loose the bonds of wickedness, to undo the heavy burdens, to let the oppressed go free, and that you break every yoke?...Then your light shall break forth like the morning, your healing shall spring forth speedily, and your righteousness shall go before you; The glory of the LORD shall be your rear guard."** (NKJV)

I want you to notice key phrases:

1. Loose the bonds of wickedness
2. Undo heavy burdens
3. Let the oppressed go free
4. Break every yoke

Each of these phrases have to do with the release of something that hinders one from experiencing the power of God, and to experience the release is not an easy thing. It is a difficult thing to do, and we can see that by the use of the words, such as bonds, burdens, oppressed, and yoke preceded by the words loose, undo, let go, and break. If we want the Spirit to operate with liberty and freedom without limits, then we are going to have to do the hard things. We are going to have to do what God instructed Jeremiah to do as noted in the following verse.

Jeremiah 1:10

> **"To root out and to pull down, to destroy and to throw down..."** (NKJV)

We have to become violent if we are to experience in a greater ever increasing level of glory and power. There can be no building and planting if there is no demolition. You cannot operate under an old order to operate within a new grace (Luke 5:36–39).

To help understand what I mean, the muscles of the body are a remarkable thing. To build muscle, you have to break it down. When you lift a weight, you work to cause the muscle to rip. When it tears, it takes a few days to build back up. When it builds back up, it grows back stronger and bigger. Thus, when you break down the flesh, the reality of expression of the spirit grows stronger and bigger. Fasting facilitates that "breaking unto building process".

These four devotionals are powerful if one does them in faith and in discipline. These devotionals are not magic, nor are they effective in producing results to the impatient. God tries our devotion over time, and the marker or measurement is faithfulness. **Constancy is key to liberty and prosperity in the gifts**. These are the building blocks to successful operation in the gifts.

The Pyramid of the Three Levels:

1. First Level – Spiritual Foundations
    *   Be Born Again
    *   Be Baptized with the Holy Spirit

2. Second Level - Spiritual Graces
    *   Grace
    *   Faith
    *   Hope
    *   Love

3. Third Level – Spiritual Devotions
   - Meditation
   - Praying in the Holy Spirit
   - Worship
   - Fasting

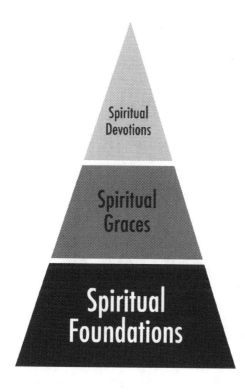

Chapter 15

Conclusion

Since we have gifts that differ according to the grace given to us, each of us is to exercise them accordingly: if prophecy, according to the proportion of his faith... (Romans 12:6-8, NASB)

In these past few chapters, I have covered what are the gifts, how to identify them, and how to operate in them. I have covered how each one is a supernatural gift, the working of the indwelling Holy Spirit, and how they manifest His presence. I have given various references to show how they are presented in Scripture, so that the reader can have a biblical reference point. I have also given some of my personal experiences in light of the gifts.

One of the major reasons why I wrote this book was so believers would begin to realize that they could operate in the gifts of the Holy Spirit. Yes, God has established the apostle, prophet, evangelist, pastor, and teacher as leaders to equip and edify the saints for the work of ministry; they are to train us to function and operate in the gifts. Certainly then, we should operate in the gifts of the Spirit. The same Holy Spirit which has been given to them to fulfill their roles has been given to Universal Church, so that the Church may fulfill its function within the world. You have a gift, and you are called to use that gift.

There is so much awaiting you as a believer in Christ. For so many years I was attending church services, yet missing out on so much more. Always at the cusp of the supernatural, but never plunging forth into the vast expanse of the river of the Spirit and the ocean of His grace. God is calling you just as He did with Peter, myself and so many others to step out of the boat of religiosity, and step into the expanse of the power of God.

The gifts are thrilling, and they bring about the realities of a living God who loves humanity so deeply that He sent His only begotten Son to die for all. The gifts are a reflection of that deep love. When you allow the Holy Spirit to work in and through you, you allow God an opportunity to express His love to another human being who is in dire need of His love. So many are love sick, and you carry the cure to what ails them – the presence and power of God administered by the Holy Spirit through love.

Just as in the parable of the talents, we must not be like the servant who took his talent, and buried it (Matthew 25:14-30). We must be like the other two servants who took their talents, and used them for the increase of their master. Christ has given us gifts, but many of us are taking them and burying them due to fear and/or an inferiority complex. There is nothing inferior to the gifts nor you. These gifts are powerful, and Satan cringes in fear at the thought of a Church where every member is operating with accuracy in the gifts. To operate in the gifts will mean that the kingdom of God will advance, and the kingdom of Satan will decrease in size and in influence (2 Samuel 3:1). Christ will be glorified, and Satan will be minimized.

To hide your talent or gift in fear is to dishonor your God and Lord, but to use your gifts will be the greatest honor. Those who honor God, He in turn will honor them (1 Samuel 2:30). God has not given you a spirit of fear, but a spirit of power, love, and of a sound mind. You have a different spirit now. You have the spirit of your Lord. You have the spirit of a lion – the lion of the tribe of Judah. Solomon says the righteous are bold as a lion, and that is you (Proverbs 28:1). Behind that persona of fear lies an untapped lion longing to come out and show the devil who is the real lion. The moment you roar by the use of the gifts, he will begin to take notice that you have just realized he is a lion without teeth. There was nothing to fear at all.

The Holy Spirit is longing within you, and His longings are:

- to manifest God to the world
- to show the world Jesus Christ is alive by the operation of the gifts
- to show forth the love of God
- to give expression to the voice of God through the gift of prophecy, tongues, and the interpretation of tongues
- to show His might by the gift of faith, the gifts of healings, and the working of miracles
- to show the world that God is infinitely knowledgeable and wise through the gifts of the word of knowledge and word of wisdom
- to show that God is the all-seeing God by the gift of the discerning of spirits

The Holy Spirit is grieved when we sin or transgress, but He is also grieved when we quench Him by spurning the gifts (1

Thessalonians 5:19-20). He has desires, but when His desires are denied or deferred, it causes Him to grieve. Why did God subject Himself to the whimsicalness

> **Love is not love if it is forced!**

of our wills? Because, love is not love if it is forced! The apostle John says in his epistle that we should not close up our hearts, but to open them (1 John 3:17). The reason is so that the love of God can flow out unhindered with freedom. When we refuse to operate in the gifts, we are closing our hearts to one another and the world. Furthermore, the Holy Spirit is affected, because He was sent into the world to convince the world of sin, judgment, and righteousness. How does He convince the world? By providing evidence! The gifts are the evidence presented in the arena of the world, so that men can be presented with the truth of the Gospel that has the power to save.

I encourage you today as you read this, do not hold back in fear, but launch out into the deep. Go beyond the shores of religion, and lose yourself in the love of God. Allow the grace of God to impact your heart and mind as the gifts operate in and through you as you hear the words of prophecy come forth through your own mouth. Hear the Spirit communicate the mind and heart of our Father who conveys His tender affection to a fellow brother or sister in Christ, or to a person who is lost in their sin. I have been privileged to hear God through prophecy convey His passion for those who were broken by sin. I have heard Him remind people of His promises that enlivened them again. It was such a powerful thing to see many fall under the power of a prophetic utterance weeping in sheer bliss and delight to know that their Father in heaven never forgot about them. The gifts are not for our entertainment, but for our edification, profit, benefit, advantage, and much more.

Let the Holy Spirit today set your heart ablaze at the thought that you too can operate in the gifts, and be used of the Master to bless people in ways that you could not naturally. God is looking for a people in this hour who will be daring to put their pride and ego aside, and to allow His Spirit to work in and through them to bless His Church, and to bless the world who needs Christ.

Will you be the one? Will you be the one in whom the Spirit can work within? I pray you are. Matter of fact, I know you are! May this book help you to launch deeper into the river of the Spirit, and be a blessing to the world.

Testimonies

Bonita

In September 2014, Elder Evans released a prophecy over me. The word of the Lord was, "Lazarus come forth." Elder Evans prophecy gave me a confirmation and a continuation of what the Lord told me 2 years before.

In May 2012, I was praying and asking the Lord what he was doing in my life as I was dealing with the chaos of my second marriage. I was unsure if that relationship would come to an end or continue. Although it was an abusive relationship, I did all I could to hold on to the marriage for fear of failure again. The word the Lord whispered to me that day was Lazarus.

I didn't completely understand what the Holy Spirit was saying at that time, but I knew it was God. So I held on to it looking to see it performed. Maybe my unbelieving husband would be truly saved. Maybe my marriage could be saved. However, in the winter of 2012 that relationship died, and ended in divorce. Then I thought maybe I would be reconciled with my first husband. Maybe that was Lazarus. And so I hoped.

I felt such guilt and shame for my failed marriages. I had faith for others and for God to move in all kinds of ways, but as for me, I had no hope of a future love. At 31, I was ashamed and embarrassed of what my family life became. In my pain I convinced myself God wanted me to live alone as a His bride forever. And all that marital failure was the evidence of that truth. I was in a crippling, hopeless death sleep, but I didn't even know it!

I remember expecting to hear a word from God that morning Elder Evans preached. When Elder delivered the prophecy over me and the Lord called 'Lazarus come forth,' I knew immediately what God was saying. Lazarus was me. And like Lazarus, the Lord was resurrecting my life and calling me out of my dark place. The Lord was freeing me from the guilt and shame, and even regret that my life decisions and failures brought me. The Lord through Elder Evans was literally cutting the chains of the pain of my past, preparing me for my future.

Since I received the prophecy, I have felt the weight of fear, regret, guilt and shame melt away. I can hold my head high and walk in freedom to live again. I am free to do the works God has called me to. I am free to receive the life and goodness that God has for me. I am even free to hope and dream of love and family again. Hallelujah Jesus!

And so to the man of God, placed in my life about 1 year ago who has patiently waited for me to respond to his desire to love me and my children, I am finally free to say yes and see what the road brings. I'm not ashamed. I'm not embarrassed. And I'm not afraid. I'm free! Praise God!

Audrey

On Sunday, September 7, 2014, Elder Evans blessed me and prophesized the following...

The Lord said, "There is a shift taking place in your life. In light of the purposes of ministry. In light of the thing of business and work and family. You are going to move and shift swiftly. So get ready for a swift transition, but also a swift blessing... I will also bring increase to your natural income... I'm going to bless you spiritually. I'm going to bless you naturally".

On September 18, 2014, I went on vacation and found myself consoling and ministering to a fellow traveler on the grace, blessings, and forgiveness of God. The ministry began.

Then in October, to my surprise, I received three awards from my employer. Two monetary awards, and a beautiful expensive desk clock from my executive vice president. A month later, in November, my manager informed me that after two years of no annual increase, I was going to receive an increase. My cup overflowed with God's blessing and his love.

It didn't stop there. I began to see and sense in the spirit. In December 2014, on two occasions the Lord Jesus visited me and made his presence known by the sweat aroma He exudes. The first time I was with my sister-in-law who's a Christian and my brother, who's a caring and hard headed man. My sister-in-law and I had just finished joyfully exalting the Lord. Then my brother smelled a sweat aroma and asked what it was. I said it was the Lord. My brother didn't believe me and thought his teenage sons had sprayed the house, but they were not home, and all the doors and windows were closed. Praise God! He is Glorious!

The second time the Lord's sweat aroma was present, I had the flu. My daughter and two sisters in Christ were praying with me. I was running fevers for three days. On the third day I was very weak and the fever peaked at 103.3. While we were praying, I saw the spirit of infirmity hovering over the door. Then it left, and I fell asleep. When I awoke, the doors and windows were closed, and I smelled the Lord's sweat aroma. The fever broke. Glory to God! His Love Never Fails!

Thank you Father, Jesus, and the Holy Spirit. Amen.

# Works Cited

Prince, Derek. *The Gifts of the Spirit: Understanding and Receiving God's Supernatural Power in Your Life*. New Kensington: Whitaker House, 2007. Print.

Cramer, Dennis. *The Master's Call: Nine Simple Questions to Identify Your Ever-Changing Call*. Cedar Rapids: Arrow Publications, 2005. Print.

Sandford, John and Paula. *The Elijah Task: A Call to Today's Prophets and Intercessors*. Tulsa: Victory House, 1977. Print.

Smith, Sean. *Prophetic Evangelism: Empowering a Generation to Seize Their Day*. Shippensburg: Destiny Image Publishers, 2004. Print.

Teleios
"Greek Lexicon :: G5321 (NKJV)." Blue Letter Bible. Sowing Circle. Web. 3 Oct, 2014. <http://www.blueletterbible.org/lang/lexicon/lexicon.cfm?Strongs=G5321&t=NKJV>.

1 Corinthians 1:4-8
"BLB - 1Co 1: Paul's Epistle - 1 Corinthians 1 (Blue Letter Bible: DBY - Darby Translation)." Blue Letter Bible. Sowing Circle.

Web. 15 Sep, 2015. <http://www.blueletterbible.orghttps://www.
blueletterbible.

Pneuma
"Greek Lexicon :: G4151 (NKJV)." Blue Letter Bible. Sowing Circle.
Web. 3 Oct, 2014. <http://www.blueletterbible.org/lang/lexicon/
lexicon.cfm?Strongs=G4151&t=NKJV>.

Python
"Greek Lexicon :: G4436 (NKJV)." Blue Letter Bible. Sowing Circle.
Web. 3 Oct, 2014. <http://www.blueletterbible.org/lang/lexicon/
lexicon.cfm?Strongs=G4436&t=NKJV>.

Pistis
"Greek Lexicon :: G4102 (NKJV)." Blue Letter Bible. Sowing Circle.
Web. 3 Oct, 2014. <http://www.blueletterbible.org/lang/lexicon/
lexicon.cfm?Strongs=G4102&t=NKJV>.

Zōopoieō
"Greek Lexicon :: G2227 (NKJV)." Blue Letter Bible. Sowing Circle.
Web. 3 Oct, 2014. <http://www.blueletterbible.org/lang/lexicon/
lexicon.cfm?Strongs=G2227&t=NKJV>.

Pantelēs
"Greek Lexicon :: G3838 (NKJV)." Blue Letter Bible. Sowing Circle.
Web. 3 Oct, 2014. <http://www.blueletterbible.org/lang/lexicon/
lexicon.cfm?Strongs=G3838&t=NKJV>.

Dunamis
"Greek Lexicon :: G1411 (NKJV)." Blue Letter Bible. Sowing Circle.
Web. 3 Oct, 2014. <http://www.blueletterbible.org/lang/lexicon/
lexicon.cfm?Strongs=G1411&t=NKJV>.

Oikodomeo

"Greek Lexicon :: G3618 (NKJV)." Blue Letter Bible. Sowing Circle. Web. 3 Oct, 2014. <http://www.blueletterbible.org/lang/lexicon/lexicon.cfm?Strongs=G3618&t=NKJV>.

Paraklēsis

"Greek Lexicon :: G3874 (NKJV)." Blue Letter Bible. Sowing Circle. Web. 3 Oct, 2014. <http://www.blueletterbible.org/lang/lexicon/lexicon.cfm?Strongs=G3874&t=NKJV>.

Paramythia

"Greek Lexicon :: G3889 (NKJV)." Blue Letter Bible. Sowing Circle. Web. 3 Oct, 2014. <http://www.blueletterbible.org/lang/lexicon/lexicon.cfm?Strongs=G3889&t=NKJV>.

Qavah

"Hebrew Lexicon :: H6960 (NKJV)." Blue Letter Bible. Sowing Circle. Web. 3 Oct, 2014. <http://www.blueletterbible.org/lang/lexicon/lexicon.cfm?Strongs=H6960&t=NKJV>.

Genos

"Greek Lexicon :: G1085 (NKJV)." Blue Letter Bible. Sowing Circle. Web. 3 Oct, 2014. <http://www.blueletterbible.org/lang/lexicon/lexicon.cfm?Strongs=G1085&t=NKJV>.

Glossa

"Greek Lexicon :: G1100 (NKJV)." Blue Letter Bible. Sowing Circle. Web. 3 Oct, 2014. <http://www.blueletterbible.org/lang/lexicon/lexicon.cfm?Strongs=G1100&t=NKJV>.

Secured Line
http://www.slideshare.net/Garry54/crypto-phones

Printed in the United States
By Bookmasters